The BRANDER -in- CHIEF™

By Joe Kiedinger

Illustrated by Amanda Dix

9th street publishing

Copies of The Brander-in-Chief are available from:

Ninth Street Publishing
321 St. George St.
Green Bay, WI 54302
www.ninthstreetpublishing.com

To inquire about Joe speaking at your next event you may contact him at 920.435.4878.

Cover art by Lisa Pritzl

Printed in the United States of America
ISBN 978-0-9821050-0-9

Published by Ninth Street Publishing
321 St. George St.
Green Bay, WI 54302
920.435.4878

Contents

I would like to thank the business leaders and mentors who let me into their lives and provided insight for my career and whose collection of wisdom helped create this book. To my parents, Tom and Barb Kiedinger: My dad taught me work ethic and emotional intelligence; my mom taught me how to engage a crowd. They both contributed to my moral code of living. To Dave Skogen, my business mentor and dear friend, who opened my eyes to the teachings of servant leadership and becoming the coach not the boss. Finally, to my beautiful wife, Danica, who began this journey with me. I appreciate your patience, personal sacrifice and support as you challenge and encourage me everyday.

Acknowledgements

Write a book? You? That was the typical response I would receive from people who have known me a long time. Once it sunk in they would say, "Cool!" You see, in college I graduated just short of a 3.0, so I certainly wasn't a stellar student. However, I loved to learn from real people who were making their dreams come true. I am easily inspired by relevant success stories. My passion for writing began in 2004 when I debuted my weekly e-newsletter, Wisdom On Wednesday. The only reason I started writing a weekly column was because of Roy Williams, a.k.a. The Wizard of Ads. He inspired me through his weekly column called Monday Morning Memo. I encourage you all to sign up for it at www.mondaymorningmemo.com.

I knew by writing weekly that it would challenge me to evaluate what I truly believe. I began my marketing career as a broadcast sales rep. It's here where I met the Skogen family and discovered their amazing grocery store, Festival Foods in Wisconsin. Dave and Mark Skogen along with COO Marlin Greenfield built me up, introduced me to Servant Leadership, and I witnessed its impact of building a solid and profitable organization. They introduced me to James Hunter, Servant Leadership guru and author of *The Servant* and *The World's Most Powerful Leadership Principle*. Dave, Mark, and Marlin encouraged me to be more than I was which led to what is now Prophit Marketing, Inc.

My new agency life introduced me to other great marketers who I studied and learned from. Nationally known experts like Ken Blanchard, Al Reis, Jack Trout and Jim Collins as well as extremely talented regional experts: Tom

Kiedinger, Robert Smith, Weston Phipps and Jim Steffel all of whom made an incredible impact on my development as a marketer.

Developing the Prophit Marketing System took a few years. What began as theory became philosophy once it was proven to work. It took faith from businesses that believed in what we were preaching. These companies have great leaders who embraced the system and executed it beautifully within their four walls. Businesses like Dahl Automotive: Harry, Andrew, Jansen and Tyler Dahl along with GM Dan Swift and Trig's Grocery stores: Trig Solberg, Lee Guenther, and Alan Alden.

I would be amiss if I didn't mention our early Prophiteers who helped build the system and our company in the early days: My wife and business partner, Danica Kiedinger, and founding members Mike Bartos and Lisa Reitz. These folks shared the struggles of both success and setbacks as we set out to discover something new.

The main character, John Kasten, is loosely based off of the inspiration I received from George Zimmer, founder and CEO of Men's Wearhouse. Mr. Zimmer granted me an interview that confirmed our system to be a solid and viable approach to marketing. Other people who had influence over the content of where the main character travels are Frank Hermans and Troy Strechenbach.

The writing and publishing of the book was a whole new support system that I truly appreciate. After doing research on book publishing and after a generous offer by HappyAbout.com to publish my book, my entrepreneurial drive told me to start my own publishing company—and 9th Street Publishing was born. The name comes from our humble beginnings. 9th Street was the home of our original office. It was located in a bedroom of a small ranch home barely 300 square feet. We never want to forget where we came from.

Three Prophiteers stepped up to get the book and publishing company off the ground: Kim Steeno, Lauren Page, and intern Katie Barlament. Together we did the research to begin a new company. We began by calling upon my friend and publisher Jim Alt. Jim gave us a quick course on publishing leading us to book layout king, Doug Hjorth. Our close friend Amanda Dix created the amazing illustrations throughout the book and Prophiteer, Lisa Pritzl, designed the stunning cover. Then I just needed to get the writing done.

I tell so many clients, "It's hard to read the label from inside the bottle," the same goes for writing. I appreciate the feedback and critique from my colleagues in business including: Larry Bilotta, Tim Solinger, Larry Desch, Bill Zeinert, and Ann Becker. Thank you to the remaining Prophiteers who do their job with excellence everyday which allowed me the time to write this book: Laurie VanDenElzen and Scott Grall.

Finally, thank you to all the successful companies who do marketing well and understand the power of a strong corporate culture. I read about you every day in trade publications and journals. You continue to inspire, which drives me to spread the good news that you can influence people and there are systems available to put yourself on the road to becoming a Brander-In-Chief.

ONCE UPON A TIME

Once upon a time… isn't that how all fairy tales start? It's also how all small businesses start. People begin with a dream and assume the "happily ever after" part will happen. Unfortunately, most small businesses never get to finish their story. These owners believed their product would be fuel enough to get them to a happy ending. Too often, that dream doesn't end happily and their business goes under.

Passion and expertise are important chapters to your story, but marketing and leadership are ultimately what give your story a plot. Furthermore, marketing isn't just a department or an aspect of business. Every decision you make is a marketing decision.

And so begins our story…

Chapter 1
ALL STRESSED OUT

Balancing the Family and the Business!

It was a cold day, even for November. Jess jumped out of her seat and yelled, "GO, Redbirds, Go… Keep driving, WHOO!" The rivalry between the East Side Redbirds and the West Side Phantoms had reached critical mass. One more victory meant playoff qualification. The score: Redbirds 7, Phantoms 13. There was less than a minute to play as the Redbirds completed their eighth play of the drive.

"Time out!" Shouted the Redbirds' coach as he called his quarterback to the sidelines with 12 seconds to play. The Redbirds were now threatening at the Phantom's 8-yard line.

Jess was on her feet along with the entire 7th Grade Booster Club as the Redbirds made their way to the line to make their final attempt. "Blue 25, Blue 25 hut, hut…" the ball was snapped from center. The quarterback faked a quick pass and pitched it to the fullback. The defense bit and committed a full pursuit to bury him. As quickly as the Phantom defense felt victorious in shutting down their opponent, their expressions switched to horror as the ball was passed over them to a wide-open tight end… touch-down!

Jess screamed with excitement along with the rest of the Redbirds' fans. Her jubilation was tempered by anxiety, though, as she knew what was to come. Her son Josh, the kicker, could win the game by kicking the extra point. Josh was a strong kicker for his age. Most kickers in the league at this age had a 60 percent success rate. Josh was becoming a star. He was one of the only kickers in his league that could kick 30-yard field goals consistently. Under this pressure, however, it would be easy to shank the kick.

Josh looked to the stands as he ran out on the field. His mother gave him a "thumbs up" for encouragement. The crowd was going crazy as the Redbirds lined up for the extra point. They were either going to be playoff bound or go into overtime.

"Green 72, Green 72… Hut…" the ball was snapped from center but was short, bouncing off the frozen tundra. Josh kept his composure and delayed his approach, if for only a fraction of a second. The ball took a lucky bounce and landed perfectly in the hands of the placeholder who spun the laces outward and held the ball in place. Josh approached the ball and gave it all he got. The ball, as if in slow motion, sailed through the goal posts sending the Redbirds to the first playoff berth in the school's history.

The Redbirds sideline went crazy. Jess, jumping up and down celebrating this amazing moment, peered in the distance to the field parking lot where she saw the blue Ford Taurus finally arrive. Disappointment, followed by anger, began to build inside her as her husband, John, walked across the parking lot to the front gate. Another family milestone missed. Like so many he missed before because of the family business.

Back at home, the tension was high. Confrontation was imminent.

"I'm sick of it, John!" Jess finally cried out, after the kids had gone to bed. "You're always working until eight or nine… when you do come home early, your mind is someplace else!"

"What do you expect!" John snapped back, "The store isn't going to run itself. If I don't do it, things don't get done!"

"Well, then maybe we should just sell it," jabbed Jess. She knew that was a real Achilles' heel for John. The idea of selling their retail business would mean failure, something that John was not capable of discussing, especially at the five-year mark. John knew that more than 50 percent of all small businesses fail within the first five years.

"Shut down the business?" John yelled back. "You know how much we've invested. We can't just close down."

"Well, I miss you, John," Jess said. "The children miss you. Josh scored the winning point and you missed it! When will that ever happen again? You should have seen the look on his face. You're missing everything! And look at these pictures Jackie drew. She's going to be an artist someday." Jess handed their daughter's drawings to John.

"Before you know it the kids will be grown and you're missing it," Jess continued, calming down and getting quietly emotional. "I feel like we're passing each other every day with the attitude, 'I'll catch up with you in 15 years.' I don't think so, John. Something must change."

Stammering in his desperation, John didn't know what to say. He had been too involved in the business. Retail is nights and weekends. Owning a men's clothing store had always been his life's ambition. He knew he was neglecting his family, yet how could he change? *It's not like the problems of the store are going away. In fact, they've grown worse as the years and marketplace has changed*, he thought.

"Things are not OK here, John," Jess said.

"I tell you what," John replied, "I'm going to cancel my hunting weekend with the boys. Let's do something together as a family."

Jane grew still. "No, I've already arranged for the

kids to stay at my mother's. Quite honestly, I need to get away myself. I'm going away for the weekend with my girlfriends."

The stress of the small business was starting to pull apart his family, and John had no idea how he could stop it. Even spending two days in a hunting lodge seemed like only a short reprieve from a life that was spinning out of control.

The following morning John packed the car, hugged his kids and headed north for the lodge.

Chapter 2
OFF TO THE LODGE

A much needed break!

John had been friends with Frank and Paul since they were kids. Paul owned Computer Troubleshooters, a business that housed 15 computer geeks. The geeks acted as the information technology departments for their clients. He also had a retail end of his business that sold computers and computer hardware. Frank owned his own flooring company. The three had been hunting together for years on the same land just 90 miles north of town.

"Man," Paul exclaimed, "business is just crankin'. We just landed several big corporate accounts. I'm surprised I was even able to get away for the weekend. How's the penguin suit business, John?"

John was used to Paul's playful joking. "Well, I

gotta be honest. I've been a little stressed out lately," John said. "It seems like the harder I work the more average my company gets."

"That's business, John. It's dog eat dog," Paul said casually.

"That's business?" John asked with sarcasm. "This is what we signed up for? Long days of tireless work! Missing dinners around the family table! Missing football games and bedtime stories! I don't know, guys. If I knew it was going to be like this when I signed up to be boss, I'm not sure I would have entered the ring," John said with a feeling of defeat.

Frank piped in then. "Ya know, John, sometimes people work themselves too hard when they're the boss. Are you sure you need to be doing everything you're doing within your business? Perhaps there are some duties you can delegate to your staff to free up some time?"

"He can't delegate," Paul interjected. "Listen, John, your employees need to remember who's the boss. Tell them what to do and watch them like a hawk. You can't trust anyone anymore to do a job right. Most of the time I just do it myself so I know it won't get screwed up."

"It seems like you guys work pretty hard then," Frank said. "I know I'm not the expert in all the aspects of my company. I try to delegate as much as possible so I only have to deal with the areas I like."

Paul shot Frank a challenging look. "So what do you delegate?"

"Billing, installation of all flooring, my information technology..." Frank said, looking at Paul with a sheepish grin.

"Ah, yeah! I love delegating... good idea, Frank, as long as you're delegating to me!" Paul teased as, his company handled all of Frank's IT services.

John reflected on this advice from his trusted friend. "That's a great point, Frank," said John. The conversation soon turned to sports and hunting, but John couldn't stop thinking of Frank's advice on the concept of delegation. That could be an important element in helping relieve his stress. The next question was, how?

Chapter 3
THE LODGE

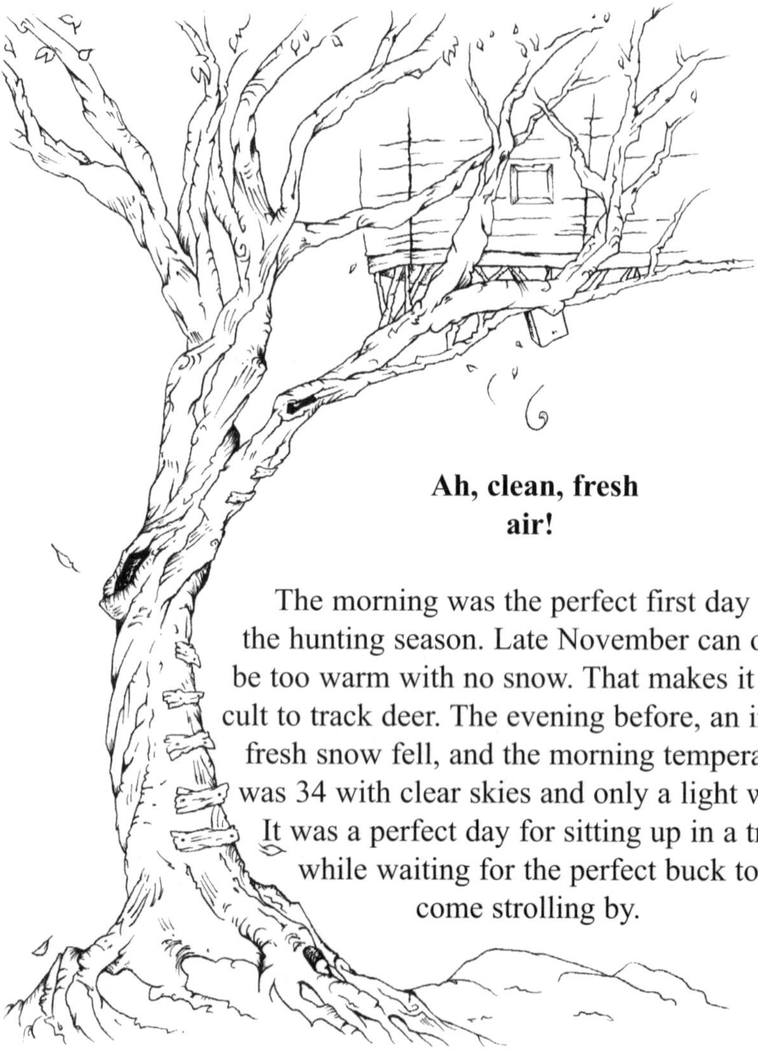

Ah, clean, fresh air!

The morning was the perfect first day of the hunting season. Late November can often be too warm with no snow. That makes it difficult to track deer. The evening before, an inch of fresh snow fell, and the morning temperature was 34 with clear skies and only a light wind. It was a perfect day for sitting up in a tree while waiting for the perfect buck to come strolling by.

After breakfast the three friends headed out into the woods. They had been hunting on Frank's land for almost 10 years now. The land belonged to his in-laws, and with more than 150 acres there was plenty of space for the three of them to spread out. Frank would always head up the week before and set up the tree stands. The spots would always be in the same area, so after 10 years they all knew exactly where each man sat. The three broke away and headed for their stands with a rifle, lunch box and thermos in hand.

John was extremely thankful that his stand was actually a spacious wooden tree fort set 25 feet high in an oak tree. He was completely concealed and had room to spread out and relax. The three of them built the tree fort on a whim eight years ago when spending a long weekend together. As he approached the tree, he inhaled deeply and tried to relax and rid his mind of the millions of thoughts running through his clouded brain. He then began to climb up the wooden planks that were nailed into the trunk of the giant oak. Every time John made this climb, he would reminisce about his childhood and all the forts he built growing up. Life was so simple back then. He approached the floor door and swung it open.

Suddenly, chaos broke out within the small chamber as John came face to face with a panicked family of raccoons. As a result of his shock, John's feet slipped off of the last plank and he started to fall. He barely managed to catch himself, as his arms were clinging to the floor with his feet and torso dangling 25 feet above the ground. He struggled to find the planks and secure his footing but his growing panic caused his weight to shift, which weakened his grip. He now realized he was about to fall 25 feet and there was nothing he could do about it. His grip then gave way. He started screaming for help but he was sure his buddies were too far away to hear his cries. And then his world went black.

Chapter 4
BRANDER-IN-CHIEF

Meet the Ad Prophet!

John slowly opened his eyes. Groggy and confused, he looked around not recognizing where he was. He found himself sitting on a white velvet chaise lounge. The room was alarmingly white, perfectly circular and appeared to have no doors or windows. Although he didn't know where he was or what was happening to him, there was a feeling of calm and normalcy to it all. Next to him sat a white high-backed leather chair. A glowingly white desk held neatly stacked white file folders, which appeared to be labeled, but he couldn't read them.

On his left, he saw a bookcase built into a significant section of the curved wall. Although it appeared to be set up like a typical bookcase with rows of books from floor to ceiling, there was definitely an orderly grouping to the books. There were seven rows to the bookcase with labels next to each row that read from the bottom up: BIC, MV, CEF, PM, MC, SOV, and P. They appeared to be acronyms for something.

John's heart jumped. Sitting on the white leather chair, which was unoccupied only a moment ago, was a man dressed in a white robe. He wore brown glasses and held a clipboard and white fountain pen.

"Good morning John, how are you feeling?" he said.

"Fine, I guess. Where am I?" John asked.

"You're in my office," said the man in white.

Then it hit him. "Oh, my God!" John exclaimed, now fully conscious and aware of what he had been through. He remembered he was going hunting and was dangling from the tree fort, lost his grip and fell. What's going to happen to my family? My kids won't have a daddy! John started to panic. "Are, are you God?"

"Oh, my no," said the man in white. "Relax, John. You are not dead, and this isn't heaven. Think of this as your wake-up call. Let me introduce myself. I am the Ad Prophet."

John's mind was spinning as he tried to sort all this out. "So you ARE sent by God!"

"No, John, I am here because of your openness to the truth. Have you ever heard of the Chinese proverb, 'when the student is ready the teacher appears'? Well, you are and I have."

"Forgive me," John replied, "but I don't understand."

The teacher went to his desk and grabbed one of the white folders and handed it to John. John read the label, "John Kasten, Brander Technician, Men's clothing store." John opened the file and saw a window-type grid. It looked like a windowpane with four equal parts. Each window had a title: Brander-In-Chief, Brander Technician, Brander Phobic, and Brander Paranoid. Inside the window was another square with John's name on it. His square was positioned with the largest percentage over the Brander Technician quadrant.

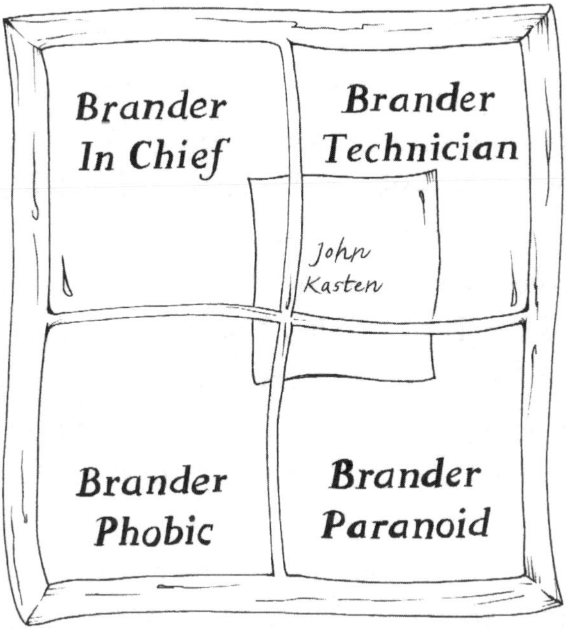

"Can you explain this?" John asked.

"What you're looking at is called a Brander Window," the Prophet said. "It reveals where the leader is at any given time. Right now, you are leading almost entirely from a Brander Technician perspective. You are doing almost everything yourself, running yourself, and your family, ragged. The goal is to lead your company as a Brander-In-Chief."

John returned to his folder. Included were seven sheets of ancient looking parchment paper. Each sheet had letters on top, but the paper was blank. He started to make the connection. The seven sheets of paper had the same letters that were labeled on the large bookcase: BIC, MV, CEF, PM, MC, SOV, and P.

"I see these pages have the same labels as your bookcase," John said.

"That's right," replied the Prophet, "You see, John, I help business owners understand how to create freedom in their lives. You work too hard, as do thousands of other small business owners. I'm going to help you work smarter—not harder. It's not too late for you. Jess deeply loves you. It's true, every person has their 'final straw,' but Jess is far from that. I've heard your desperation and I'm going to help you get your life and business back on track."

"He knows my wife's name?" John thought to himself.

"I'm going to teach you my fail-proof marketing system. But, you must first become a prophet to make a profit," the Prophet said. "With the proper coaching, you will gain back time with your family while growing your business. Would that be of interest to you?"

John thought that even if this was all a dream he'd go along with it. "If you can show me how to do that, I'll be forever in your debt," he said enthusiastically.

"Let's get started. The first lesson you need to know is this: Every business decision you make is a marketing decision—who you hire, who you fire, which capital improvements, advertising options. Every decision you make is a marketing decision. With that being said, I have developed seven key areas that successful companies, big and small, have working for them to help them be successful. I am going to reveal them to you. These seven ingredients are presented in rows on the bookshelf and in your folder. Let's get started. What does that first label read on the first sheet in your folder?" asked the Prophet.

"It says BIC," John replied.

"That stands for Brander-In-Chief," the Prophet said, "and it's the ultimate goal you need to seek. To be a Brander-In-Chief you need to be involved in your marketing and you need to lead your associates with authority, not power."

"What is your leadership style, John?" the Prophet asked.

"I don't know. I've never really thought about it," John said. "I guess I tell my people what I expect from them and make sure they do it."

"No, you don't," the Ad Prophet stated curtly. "You're telling me what you'd like me to think. You don't actually do what you just said."

"Are you calling me a liar?" John replied somewhat offended.

"Not at all. It's just that most business owners look at the world through rose-colored glasses rather than clear honesty about how they lead their organization," said the robed one succinctly.

"Let's take a test, fair enough?" the Prophet said.

"Sure," replied John cautiously.

"You claim to tell your people what you expect of them and make sure they follow through. Is that correct?"

"Well, yeah," John said hesitantly.

"See this? Do you know what it is?" the Prophet said holding out what appeared to be a walking stick.

John studied it carefully. "It looks like an ornately carved walking staff that appears to have come right out of the movie, *The Ten Commandments*," he said. It was hand-carved and on top was a money sign.

"It's a prophit staff, John. This staff allows you to look at yourself from the outside. Sometimes, we get so inside the bottle we can't read our own label. Grab the staff with me, John, and close your eyes, but don't open them until I tell you. Do you understand?"

"Yes," John replied.

John closed his eyes and in a few moments he received his instruction to open them. They had been transported to his own store. They stood in his office, and before them was John with an associate. He was giving an annual performance review.

"That's Laurie. She's one of our tailors," John said. The calendar on the wall indicated this review happened three months ago.

The teacher whispered to John, "listen to yourself." John stared at the ongoing review almost in disbelief.

"So, Laurie," John asked, "how's everything going?"

"Fine," Laurie responded. "I have no complaints. Everything seems to be running smooth."

"Good to hear, Laurie. Are you double-stitching the hems on all the pants?" John said.

"No." Laurie answered cautiously.

"I've been checking over your work, specifically the hems you have sewn. Are you satisfied with them?" he asked.

"Well, yes, why… is there something wrong?" replied Laurie.

"Oh no," John said. "I just wouldn't have done it that way. I typically double-stitch to make sure the hems don't fall. You should try and double-stitch when you can."

The remainder of the conversation consisted of chatting about her family and social life. The whole meeting was about a half hour and had no real substance.

John's face turned red. He felt embarrassed by his lack of leadership in that scenario. He suddenly realized he was now sitting in the chaise lounge back in the Ad Prophet's office.

"Your coaching style is vague at best, John. The problem with young leaders is they don't know how to correct and discuss behavior that needs repair," the Prophet said. "If your system of double-stitching hems is superior, then that's how everyone should do it. You need to make it clear so Laurie can follow the standards of the organization. The Brander-In-Chief develops a system for 'this is how we do it here,' communicates the standards and holds his people accountable. Accountability is the essence of leadership. Your associates spend the majority of their waking hours under your care. It's up to you to grow them into better employees."

"I admit I don't like confrontation," John said humbly.

"No one does," the teacher replied. "But if you signed up to be the leader, you need to set the expectation. Identify the gap between how you wish a person to perform and how they are currently performing. Discuss how they will eliminate that gap."

The teacher continued. "There are four types of Branders who run a business: The Brander Technician, The Brander Paranoid, the Brander Phobic and the Brander-In-Chief."

"According to my folder, I'm a Brander Technician." John held up his folder and pointed to the Brander Window.

"Most fledgling business owners are Brander Technicians," the Ad Prophet said, "You are really good at what you do. You've always excelled at fashion retail, specifically men's clothing. You're an excellent tailor, so you started your own store. The problem is the Technician does everything, often running around the business like a lost puppy. You wear too many hats and insist on approving every little detail. Therefore, you fear losing control, and it consumes you. You are involved in everyone's business, but ultimately you lose control. It's a double-edged sword."

"That's me, alright." John said. "My dad always preached that the only way to make it was to be your own boss and to work hard day in and day out."

"Perhaps you should consider working smarter not harder," the Prophet said. "As a Brander-In-Chief, you must develop a system that your people can follow. The system will set you free. You can count on it."

"Let's take a moment to briefly go over the other Brander types, John. First, there is the Brander Paranoid. They're the most difficult. These leaders, and I use that term loosely, surround themselves with 'yes' people. They typically hire those less capable than they are so that they can feed their own egos. Then, they can prove they know the most and that they're always right."

John paused for a moment and thought. "Man, that sounds like my buddy Paul." He said.

"The computer guy," the Prophet said as if he and

Paul had been friends for years.

"So, you know him? Did he fall out of a tree, too?" John said.

"No," chuckled the teacher. "Paul may never be ready for me to appear, take a look." The Ad Prophet fingered through the stack of white folders on his desk and tossed one to John, who quickly identified the words on the tab: Paul Barenson – Brander Paranoid.

"Besides," the teacher went on, "a Brander Paranoid thinks they ARE a Brander-In-Chief. They typically are very involved in their advertising and marketing, but they fail to trust the people they partner with and therefore change their minds often. They can never stay true to a theme or campaign because if they don't see an immediate response every time, they decide it's not working, which in most cases just isn't true. They are closed minded and opinionated, which destroys reaching their true potential. Their overall philosophy is: "I don't trust you and never will!"

John fell back in his chair thinking about his friend Paul. "Is there any hope for the Brander Paranoid?" John asked.

"There's always hope," the Prophet said encouragingly, "but they need to learn to trust and empower people first. A very difficult programming change for the Brander Paranoid."

"The third type of Brander is the Brander Phobic. I know the word 'phobic' has a negative connotation, but the

Brander Phobic is wonderful at delegating. The problem is that sometimes they delegate a job to the wrong person. They know they need marketing, for example, so they tell their administrative assistant, who they know had one marketing class in college, that they will field all marketing phone calls. Meanwhile, their assistant is all stressed out with a responsibility they are not qualified to assume. So, they know how to delegate, but don't always delegate to the right people."

John started to connect the dots. "Frank, my buddy Frank talks about partnering with people when it comes to different areas of his business. Is he a Brander Phobic?"

"Let's see," said the Ad Prophet as he rummaged through his file folders. "Ah, yes, here we are." He tossed Frank's file over to John. "Take a look at his Brander Window."

John looked at the title: Frank Stone – Brander Phobic. He opened the folder and pulled out the Brander window diagram. Frank's window was split between Brander-In-Chief and Brander Phobic.

"There's a big difference between having Brander-In-Chief qualities and living like a Brander-In-Chief," the Ad Prophet said.

"The coveted position is that of the Brander-In-Chief, or BIC," the teacher said triumphantly. "First, the BIC is involved in the advertising and marketing of the company. Every piece of communication that goes out has the BIC's thumbprint on it. The second biggest difference: the BIC creates friction every now and then."

John looked at the Prophet somewhat confused. “I like harmony in my work place. Friction is uncomfortable. It’s so hard to find good people, and I don’t want them looking for employment elsewhere,” he said.

“Friction can be bad, John, but not all friction is bad,” the Prophet said. “Holding people accountable to the organization and to each other is the essence of leadership. You’re not going to grow them if they’re not held accountable. It’s too bad that most company leaders don’t always know how to confront associates. Create a transparent organization. Allow information to flow freely creating a secure environment where you hold your people accountable, and, conversely, they are allowed to hold you accountable as well. You’re their coach. Don’t just give feedback in the yearly review. Feedback is a weekly thing and should be provided on an ongoing basis.”

“When you see a person under-performing, approach him or her one-on-one and start your conversation like this: ‘I need to be real with you right now.’ Educate your people that when anyone begins a conversation in this way they are to give their full attention. They are to not get defensive. They need to hear what is about to be said. On the flip side, when you see an associate over deliver on a task, praise them in front of your whole organization.”

It was clear what the teacher was saying and John realized he needed to do a better job of leading his team and holding them accountable.

"Take a look at the BIC sheet in your folder," the Prophet instructed.

John pulled out the sheet titled BIC. The page, which was blank a few moments ago, now was filled with notes. "The fundamental beliefs that guide a Brander-In-Chief are on your sheet. Let's go through them," the Prophet said.

Work ON your business not IN your business

"The BIC works ON the business not IN it. Do you understand what I'm saying here, John?" the Prophet asked.

"I suppose you're not referring to this past summer when I tried to fix the air conditioning unit on top of my building?" John mused.

"Not particularly," the teacher smiled, "Right now, you are a Brander Technician. You do almost everything yourself including ordering, payroll, accounting and even sales. You name it, you do it."

"Ah, yeah, that's right," John replied as if every entrepreneur thought this way.

The Prophet walked over to the wall, behind his desk. He then pulled out a marker from his robe and began writing on the perfectly spotless colorless wall. He created a football play with X and O markings to represent offense and defense.

"You need to be the coach, John, not the boss. Your players are the ones who win the game. It's your job to call the plays so the players know what to do. Here's another way of thinking about this: Your success will not be judged on what you get done, but what you get done through others. That means you need to delegate. Who's going to be your quarterback, running back and receiver? Teach them your system of 'this is how we do it here' and be relentless in coaching them to be their best. You need to delegate your busy work so you can be the coach. This is done by hiring people who are smarter than you in their respective position in the business. It will set you free and is the fundamental fabric of all Brander-In-Chiefs. A BIC has fundamental beliefs that help to guide his decisions," the Prophet said.

Understand that a great brand is in it for the long haul

"People's lives are filled with distraction," the Prophet said. "Your customers have children, sporting practices to get them to, and other activities to coordinate. They have jobs that have deadlines. They have stress to deal with. On top of it all, they have social lives they're trying to maintain. Prospects do not have time for you to figure out who you are. The Brander-In-Chief understands this and is consistent with everything they do, from the customer experience within their four walls to the advertising message they promote."

"Conversely, the Brander Paranoid will try something for six months. When it appears to not be working to his expectations, he'll change directions. But the Brander-In-Chief will stay the course for years building a brand people understand and rely on."

Establish a consistent Customer Experience Factor through systems of "this is how we do it here"

"The BIC believes the system is the solution when it comes to creating a consistent experience for the customer," the Prophet said. "This means the staff knows what is expected, whether it's how the phones are to be answered, how customers are to be serviced, or what the follow-up procedures are for handling complaints. The goal should be 100 percent compliance by everyone so they execute the system every day. This gives the leader peace of mind knowing the customer experience will be consistent from visit to visit."

Practice what you preach

"So, now you've created this system," the Prophet said. "If your associates don't see you setting your own system in motion through your actions, then it will collapse. You must lead by example not by instruction. You then remind over and over again so it becomes a habit."

Hold your people accountable

"If associates go outside the system, they need to be approached immediately and reminded about the 'this is how we do it here' system," the Prophet continued. "By not holding your people accountable, you are condoning actions that go against the system and destroy the consistency of the customer experience. Also, be open-minded when an associate points out a behavior of yours that may have strayed from the procedures of the system. Thank them for being truly good team players."

Practice the teachings of Servant Leadership

"You need to be a student of Servant Leadership," the Prophet said.

John interrupted. "Isn't that biblically based?"

"You're right," the Prophet said. "Over 2,000 years ago, historical accounts of Jesus had him teaching Servant Leadership to his apostles. He said if you wish to be the leader, you first must serve. Servant Leadership is described in two words. The first is Servant. The Servant meets the legitimate needs of his or her people. The second, Leadership, means to lead with authority. Leading by authority means people are following you because they want to. Do you know what the opposite of authority is, John?"

"Ah, not really," John responded.

"Power," the Prophet clarified. "Power is getting people to do what you want out of fear. Do it or else. Authority is getting people to follow you because they feel a part of your vision and they trust you as their leader. They believe in the direction and the goals you are striving for and they take on those goals as their own. It's kind of like your associate is driving a car and you're asking them to drive as fast as they can from point A to point B. The road is full of speed bumps, and in order for them to achieve the time goals of the drive you must remove those speed bumps. That's where the Servant comes in. You remove all obstacles, which is what they need to be able to efficiently complete the trip."

Be involved in marketing decisions

"The BIC doesn't necessarily develop the marketing strategy or write the ad copy," continued the Prophet. "They hire people with talent and experience who dedicate time to this crucial business element. The BIC looks at every piece of marketing information to make sure it properly represents the company's vision and Mantra."

"What's a Mantra?" John asked.

"We'll get to that," replied the Prophet. "The point is, nothing goes out without the BIC's approval. It's crucial that you are involved in how your company is being presented internally and externally."

Execution: Intention + Action = WILL

"BICs are great at executing whatever initiatives they wish to engage," the Prophet told John. "They execute their vision through others. They are involved because they provide direction, guidance and feedback. But the glory comes in seeing others take action and excel. You never hear a BIC talk about themselves when discussing success. They always give the credit to others. So many business owners have wonderful intentions, but there is rarely any action. Therefore nothing happens. The biggest problem for most leaders is their inability to delegate and communicate their vision. A BIC constantly reminds the troops about the vision of the organization."

If you're going to lead you've got to read

"BIC's believe in Prophet Thinking. That is you must become a prophet to make a profit. Others have taken the entrepreneurial journey before you. Learn from them. You must seek out information at all times from people who are smarter than you. Read, go to seminars and continually better yourself intellectually on a regular basis," the Ad Prophet said.

John looked overwhelmed. "There's so much to know. How can I hear your words and suddenly become a Brander-In-Chief. It just seems overwhelming?"

"This is a journey of becoming, John," the Prophet

said. "No one expects you to magically transform years of bad habits. Keep these philosophies handy to remind you every day. If you're going to lead you've got to read. The world keeps changing. Continuous education is crucial for the Brander-In-Chief."

BiC

The Brander-in-Chief Code of Leadership

Work ON your business not
IN your business.

Understand that a great brand is in it
for the long haul.

Establish a consistent Customer Experience
Factor through systems of
"this is how we do it here".

Practice what you preach.

Hold your people accountable.

Practice the teachings of
Servant Leadership.

Be involved in marketing decisions.

Execution: Intention + Action = WILL

If you're going to lead you've
got to read.

Chapter 5
MARKET VIABILITY

Find your niche!

"Let's move on," the teacher said. "Please give me the letters on the next page in your folder."

John placed the BIC page to the back of his folder and grabbed the next blank sheet. "It says MV," John said.

"M-V, that's Market Viability," the Ad Prophet explained. "It has two meanings. First, is your company—what it offers, how it offers it, and how it makes that offer viable within your market conditions. Are there a large number of men's clothing stores in your market area? Are you conducting your business reflecting today's lifestyle needs? Have you properly identified those needs? Your niche within your product category is what keeps you a viable business in the future."

"Don't I have a niche?" John asked. "I have men's clothing from casual to suits?"

"That is where you struggle, John," the Prophet said. "You do have a distinct position in the clothing category because you serve only men. However, there are other men-only clothing stores, am I right?"

"Well, yeah, I have about eight other main competitors," John replied.

"Because you are a Brander Technician, you have this fundamental belief that 'if you build it they will come,' " the Prophet said. "You must look further and create a *relevant* niche within your men's clothing store category that consumers can understand. When it comes to that niche, customers will think of you first. You have limited your niche to serve only men. That is a good start, but you must take it a step further. Come with me to the bookcase. Take a look at the title of the books on the shelf titled MV."

John crouched down looking over the first row of books labeled BIC. They were literally on the floor. These books were all leadership titles: *Leading with Authority - Not Power, Needs VS. Wants, The Great Art of Influence, Dancing with your Dreams,* and many more. The second row was labeled MV. The titles of some of these books included: *Pizza, Ice Cream, Sporting Goods, Sandwiches, Fast Food, Shampoo.*

"They appear to all have a general industry or product as the title," John observed.

"That's right, grab one," the Prophet instructed.

John grabbed *Fast Food* and opened it. He opened the book. Although the book appeared from the outside to be thick and full of pages, it was relatively simple when opened. Each page had a fast food restaurant name on it.

"Give me the restaurant on the first page," the Prophet said.

"OK, Taco Bell," John said.

"What do you think of when you think of Taco Bell?" the Prophet asked.

"Tacos and burritos. Mexican food in a hurry," John quickly replied.

"You see! Your brain knew in a moment what that name represented," the Prophet said. "Give me the next three along with your quick understanding of the brand."

"OK." John was beginning to get into this. "KFC-fast food chicken, Colonel Sanders. Next page, I see McDonalds, the best known of the burger and fry chains." John easily was able to express the niche of each brand represented.

"Do you see how quick your mind could tell me their unique position in the fast food marketplace?" said the Prophet as he grabbed a book off the shelf titled *Shampoo.* "Now, John, I want you to tell me the top three shampoo brands that jump into your mind."

John wasn't a big shampoo connoisseur. "Let's see… Prell, Herbal Essence, my wife uses that, and… Suave. Wow, that was hard for me," John said.

"Let me make it easier for you," the teacher chimed

in. "What is the first dandruff shampoo that jumps into your mind?"

"Head and Shoulders!" John shot out.

"Great," the teacher chuckled as he saw John's total immersion into this important exercise. "How about a baby shampoo?"

"Johnson and Johnson! Is there any other?"

"Why yes, John, there are. Matter of fact, there are dozens of brands of baby shampoo on the market today. Johnson and Johnson has been consistent in its pursuit to remind you that they are THE baby shampoo. Baby shampoo is an interesting one because for years you've seen ads for Johnson and Johnson baby shampoo, and there was never a need. But your brain filed it away and pulled it out when your son was born."

"You see, John, with both the fast food and shampoo examples, the companies that have created an association and that have stayed consistent in their advertising message have reserved the space in your brain for that category."

The light bulb went on for John. He was so excited he wanted to go through more books, but by now he could predict what he would find in each and every book - a bunch of niches! He had to search deep to find a niche that he could satisfy within the men's clothing market. More than ever, he appreciated that he could at least say he focused exclusively on men's clothing. He was on the right track and knew he could take it to the next level.

"In my business, how could I create an even bigger niche?" John asked.

"Well, only you can answer that. It starts by looking at your competition," the Prophet said. "Usually, there's no room to be a 'me too' company. How are your competitors under serving the market within your product category? How can you better offer that service within your own four walls? A niche typically lies in one of these categories: service, price, selection or shopping experience… It's up to you."

"When you say 'shopping experience,' do you mean customer service?" John asked. In his clothing store, the sales people take care of the customer by helping them make selections, but when he heard the Prophet say "shopping experience" he felt there was something more to it.

"John, I'm not talking about giving the customer a service. Everyone does that," the Prophet said. "I'm talking about giving the customer a 'WOW, that felt great, I'm telling everyone I know'… EXPERIENCE! The greatest entrepreneurs create impact with people by offering them a memorable experience that happens when a customer is interacting with their brand. Your advertising might get them in, but *only* the Customer Experience Factor can make them raving fans."

MV

Market Viability

1. There are riches in niches. What's yours?

2. When you have a niche customers
think of you first.

3. What position will you maintain within your product
category that will be understood
by your prospects?

4. Don't be a 'Me Too' company.

Chapter 6
CUSTOMER EXPERIENCE FACTOR

Meet a Brander-In-Chief

"Time to take another trip," the Prophet said as he motioned for John to grab the staff.

"Where are we going this time?" John asked.

"To meet a genuine Brander-In-Chief and explore the positive influence of a high Customer Experience Factor. It's the next phase of great marketing. Close your eyes and hold on."

When John opened his eyes he was standing outside of what appeared to be a grocery store. The outside of the building looked friendly and inviting. The store was called Jack's Place, and a large golden stake was mounted on the outside wall near the entrance. On the stake was a sign that read:

> "*You're our number one priority. We've staked everything on it." — Jack*

They stepped inside, and John was blown away. It was the most beautiful grocery store he had ever seen. The first department they entered was Produce. They stood among the most amazing fruit and vegetable displays, which were made even more spectacular by the store's impeccably polished floors.

"Good morning," an employee said to John and the teacher. "Can I help you find anything?"

"Ah, good morning," John replied. "We're just looking."

The employee then looked at the Prophet. "Oh, hello Stewart! Looking for Jack?"

"Actually, we are. Is he up in his office?" The Prophet replied.

"You know Jack, he's on the floor *inspecting what he expects.* He could be bagging, coaching an associate or kissing babies for all I know. He's around. Would you like me to page him?"

"That's alright," the Prophet said. "We're not in a hurry. Besides, my friend John and I would like to take a look around anyway."

"Well then, John, enjoy your visit," the employee said.

"Thanks, ah, Tim" John said reading the employee's name tag.

"My pleasure," Tim replied.

"Stewart!" John said. "Your name is Stewart!" A triumphant feeling overcame him as he discovered the information that would humanize his new mentor. *I finally know his name*, John thought.

"I wasn't hiding it. You simply never asked me. You can certainly call me Stewart. In fact, I'd prefer it."

"So… Stewart, why are we here?" John asked. He somehow felt more connected with his new teacher now that he knew his name.

"To learn from one of the greatest Brander-In-Chiefs I know. This is Jack's Place," Stewart said.

"That's a strange name for a grocery store," John replied.

"Is it?" Stewart asked. "Jack understands that there are two places a person spends most of their time. The first being at their place of employment, the other is at home. Then there is that third place. It might be a local coffee shop for some or a grocery store for others. Jack realized people spend a considerable amount of time at the grocery store, sometimes visiting three or more times every week.

It often becomes their third place."

John deduced the rest. "So, he called the third place *Jack's Place*."

"You got it!" Stewart nodded.

Continuing on through the store, they passed through the produce section and John spotted a high-definition TV monitor. On the monitor there were children playing in a colorful room.

"What is that?" John asked.

"That is a supervised children's play area," Stewart replied. "It's a place where parents can leave their children so they can take their time shopping. These monitors are throughout the store so parents can observe their child while they shop."

"Clever," John said. "How long can the kids stay there?"

"As long as needed to complete their shopping," said Stewart as he continued past the monitor to the next area of Jack's Place.

Just ahead were the deli, hot food, salad and sushi bars. As they approached the deli, a friendly associate shouted out, "Pound of smoked turkey!" The other four associates behind the case yelled back, "Pound of smoked turkey!" The deli clerk quickly handed the wrapped smoked turkey to a female customer in her late twenties with a 2-year-old child attached to her hip. *Obviously, this child wasn't fond of leaving mom behind and sitting in childcare*, thought John.

"Maybe this will help," said the service-case clerk as she offered a large cookie.

"For me?" asked the young mom. "No, we'll be fine."

"Please take it," the smiling deli clerk said. "It's on Jack."

"Well, thank you so much. I'll have to thank Jack the next time I see him," the woman said.

John noticed the child's eyes open wide as she fixated on the cookie. The mom placed her daughter in the seat of the shopping cart. The child clutched the cookie and chomped into it, no longer needing the hip that moments ago was a priority.

"The system here includes being aware of customers who may need assistance," Stewart explained. "The deli associate saw a child creating some discomfort for mom so she stepped in to relieve that stress with a simple cookie."

The rest of the store experience was similar. Customers were smiling and enjoying their shopping experience. Grocery associates were seen walking customers to items they couldn't find. Conversations between employees and customers were commonplace. It appeared to John that everyone actually enjoyed grocery shopping. Could it be? There was even a bistro-like setting with twinkling lights and plants near the deli area where couples and friends could enjoy a latte and chat before completing their shopping. There was even an area for customers to park their carts while they were lounging.

John and Stewart then moved on to the bakery where they were greeted by the smell of freshly-baked bread. Another smiling associate came up to them with a freshly cut slice.

"Care to sample some Italian wheat? Oh, hi Stewart!" the bakery worker said.

"Hi, Kim," Stewart responded. "We would love some."

Directing her attention to John, she said, "Hi, I'm Kim. Welcome to Jack's Place. I hope you're finding everything you've been looking for. Seeing how you have no cart, I can only assume you're here looking for Jack."

"We are, actually. I'm John. Your store is wonderful and so is this bread," John replied.

"I see you're married" Kim said, observing John's wedding ring. If you really want to earn points with the wife, take home some of this balsamic oil to dip the bread along with a bottle of red," said Kim. "I suggest the Ordahl Estate Cellars Merlot or Cabernet. You can't go wrong."

"I'll remember that. Thanks for the tip." John said.

As Kim made her way to the next guest, John turned to Stewart. "She is sincerely delightful!"

"Yes, she is. If you didn't notice, she tried to cross-sell you three different products by pairing them: bread, oil and wine," Stewart said. "Because you were engaged in conversation, you didn't even realize it. Pairing is part of the system Jack put in place."

"How is it possible that everyone is so charming and personable?" John asked. "If I could get my people to behave this way I'd be a millionaire!"

"You hit the nail on the head—behavior is the key word!" Stewart said rejoicing. "They see Jack behaving this way. They see all the upper management behave this way day after day. The associates understand that if they want to be a part of this 'Jack's Place' experience, they'll need to live out the 'this is how we do it here' customer experience."

As they continued on, the checkouts came into view. Stewart looked at John and said, "Ah, there he is."

John realized that 'he' meant Jack, so John started looking for a man in uniform talking with an employee or running hurriedly around the front of the store. "I don't see him," John said.

"There," Stewart said. "Checkout lane number five."

"All I can see is a checker and a bagger," John said.

Stewart chuckled. "Jack *is* the bagger!"

John was astounded. Here was a smiling man in his mid-60s bagging the groceries of an elderly woman. He held her attention with interesting conversation.

Shouldn't he be managing the store? John thought. As they approached, the woman looked at Jack and thanked him warmly for the help. "My pleasure, Susan.

Say 'hi' to Bob," Jack said to the woman. "Tell him there's no way the Cardinals aren't going to the World Series this year."

"You'll have to tell him that yourself. I stay out of your sports battles," the woman replied.

Jack laughed as the two finished their dialogue. Soon Jack turned his attention to Stewart and John.

"Stewart!" exclaimed Jack as he and Stewart formed their hands into fists as if rehearsed and bumped them together.

"Great to see you, Jack!" Stewart said. "I would like to introduce you to my latest student, John Kasten."

"Hello, John. Pleasure to meet you." Jack said with a twinkle in his eye.

"Your store is incredible, Mr...," John wasn't sure how to address him.

"You can call me Jack, and I appreciate your comment," Jack told John. "We work hard to make sure it's the best shopping experience around."

John noticed that Jack was dressed like the other store managers. He wore a nice pressed blue shirt with a nametag that said 'Jack,' and he wore a whistle around his neck.

"Perhaps we could steal away to your office, Jack, and share some quality time, if it's the right time," Stewart suggested.

"Love to," Jack said. Before he left, Jack made sure another smiling associate covered his bagging station.

The three headed up a black staircase to the upstairs offices. As they were about to step into Jack's office, John noticed a sign just to the right of the door. It read:

"Please check your worries at the door.
This is a safe place."
— Jack

"So, John, what do you like about the store and what can we do better?" asked Jack. John wasn't expecting this line of questioning; he was caught off guard, which actually helped him produce an honest response.

"As we shopped your store, I noticed everything was virtually spotless," John said. "The floors, the various departments and the deli and meat cases were all impeccably fresh. Also, everyone was so friendly… genuinely so. I heard a lot of 'my pleasure' and watched employees walk customers to items they couldn't find. I'm not used to this kind of treatment from the store in my neighborhood."

"Thank you for that, John." Jack said, "This experience didn't happen by itself. We had a serious plan on how to create this service culture. We pride ourselves on it. We understand the customer cuts our paychecks. Without them, it's curtains."

"How do you do it? What's the secret?" John asked, searching for the one bit of advice that would transform his business. *If he could create this kind of culture at his store, the cash registers would be ringing nonstop,* he thought.

"Let me ask you a question, John," Jack said. "Are you passionate about what you do?"

"Absolutely," John replied. "I've been in the retail clothing business all my life. I couldn't imagine doing anything else."

"That's good," Jack confirmed. "Do you feel as if you're running the store by the seat of your pants?"

"Yeah, I do." John replied embarrassingly. "I want to change but I don't know how. I don't feel in control of my destiny. I just get through day by day praying that sales will beat expenses and that no one hands me their two-week notice."

"There is definitely a secret to Jack's Place that's not happening in the four walls of your business, John," Stewart said. "Not everyone is ready to hear it, but I think you are." Stewart looked at Jack and nodded.

"Now, son," Jack said, "if you are to become privy to this information you need to work it. Understand, there is no pixie dust here that's going to fix your organization. Once you're given the secret you need to internalize it, then apply it. Intention without action is nothing. You understand?"

"I appreciate you taking the time to teach me the secret to building an exceptional business. I will apply it. You have my word," John said respectfully.

Jack got up and headed to a painting on the wall. He removed the painting and behind it was a wall safe. *This was like a scene right out of a spy thriller*, thought John. Jack made several quick spins with the dial, which resulted in the safe's steal door suddenly popping open. Inside were two boxes. The first was a shiny gold box. It was rather small - like a box a watch would come in. The second was no ordinary box. John recognized it immediately as Jack removed it from the safe and extended it to him. It was a McDonald's Happy Meal TM box.

"The secret lies within. It's my gift to you," Jack said almost reverently.

John looked at Stewart who nodded approvingly. *Are they kidding?* John wondered. He gently reached for the package that he hoped held the answers he had so long been yearning for. Is it possible that inside could be the answer of running a successful, stress-free business? Could it be that inside was the future that would allow more time at home with his family while building a successful enterprise? Although he wanted to laugh at the presentation of the box, it was clear that Jack and Stewart were taking this seriously. He slowly opened the Happy Meal box and saw inside a small red piece of silk material about three inches long. John pulled it out. There were five words in yellow transcribed on the silk. It read:

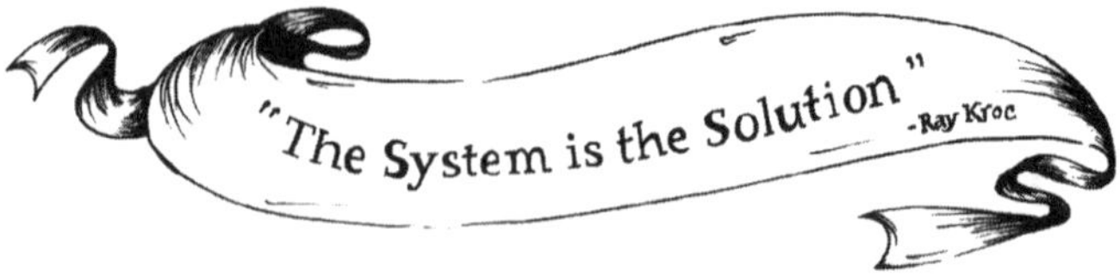

"I don't understand," John said.

"Ray Kroc, founder of the McDonald's franchise believed that the system of running a McDonald's restaurant was more important than the products themselves, everything from timed cooking of burgers and fries to the drive-up window." Jack explained. "Ray set out to create a restaurant where the system of operations was so turnkey that a 19-year old kid could operate it. Ray never flipped a burger himself. Once he got the system right, he invited people to come see it and sold thousands of franchises. You know the rest of the story. That is why the McDonald's customer experience is the same wherever you go. A Big Mac is a Big Mac whether purchased in Wisconsin or Nebraska."

"In order to create a positive culture in your organization you must understand the system your organization will run on," Stewart said in an evangelical tone. "It's a proven plan, a 'this is how we do it here' culture. The system helps business owners stay on course with what is important in establishing and sustaining a successful business that works for the owner, even when the owner is not there."

"You see, John," Jack took over, "you must become a prophet to make a profit. Prophet Thinking is learning from other great entrepreneurs that came before you. You see, the prophet is first the student and then becomes the teacher."

John reflected on everything he had seen and heard so far in this surreal experience.

"All those labels in my folder and on the book shelves-they're all stages of a system?" he asked.

"Yes, my protégé, a system that will set you free. Right now we're discussing the third piece to the system, the Customer Experience Factor," Stewart reminded him.

"My family created a Constitution of how we do things here," Jack interjected. "Each one of us lives and breathes this Constitution every day. The reason you see our associates meet and greet customers is because they see us doing it. We remind them daily that 'this is how we do it here.' Eventually they begin following our system. Over time, a healthy culture is born. We sell the same bottle of catsup in our store as the competitor down the street. Therefore, we need to give the customer other reasons to shop us."

"So, how long does it take to create a WOW customer experience?" John asked.

"It depends how clearly you visualize your system and communicate it to your associates," Jack responded. "It isn't easy. You need to get your box organized before you can start seeing positive change. By box, I mean within the four walls of your business. The biggest killer of business is inconsistency. You need to get specific as to how you do things. Then, you must hold people accountable to those beliefs, values and systems. You should get your employees involved in helping you create that 'Wow Experience' together. Being the leader means that you create buy-in from your people. It's not your company—it's everyone's company."

"You mean let the inmates run the prison?" John asked.

"No," corrected Stewart. "It means you need to get your people involved. Explain how they fit in the organization as a contributor and empower them to help create your constitution. It's then your job as the BIC to make sure they stick to it everyday."

"The system gives you freedom," Stewart continued. "You need to create a system of how to run your business day to day. Make it so simple that you could teach a 19-year-old kid who has an interest in retail how to do it. The system dictates how people are to act, how customers are greeted, how customer complaints are to be handled. The values of your company should be clearly presented. Everyone needs to understand the knowledge of your system. It is your 'this is how we do it here' approach to business. They also need to know what will happen if they don't adapt to this system. When your system is understood by your associates, you will have a presence even when you are not present!" John had to think about that one.

"The hardest part isn't creating the system but the relentless pursuit of sticking to it, day after day, month after month, year after year." Jack said. "Holding people accountable is your number one job. I wear this whistle around my neck to remind my associates that I'm their coach. The coach's job is to raise the game of all the players. They may not like you all the time, but they'll love you *over time*."

"Create a culture where employees feel comfortable approaching you to raise your game as well," Jack continued. "They have every right to approach you with issues they're concerned about. You're the leader, John. You need to be approachable. Your goal is to create total consistency of experience for the people writing your paycheck - the customer."

John felt somewhat overwhelmed, but truly inspired. "So, your business is based on your golden stake message I read outside at the entrance of the store?" John surmised.

"That's right," Jack said, "We've staked everything on delivering only the best customer experience. Seriously, if this didn't work, we would lose everything, and my associates know that. I remind them often. Therefore, every decision I make is based on delivering on that promise, including who we hire and who we fire, to the vendors we work with and the equipment we choose to upgrade.

Every decision must go back to that promise. Your experience needs to be unique in today's business world. Giving customers what they expect is mandatory. But exceeding their expectation pays dividends. The system we put in place guides our associates in delivering an experience unmatched by our competition: treating our guests to a 'WOW' experience every time they enter the store."

"But how did you start putting this system together? I don't know where to begin!" John asked with a hint of exasperation.

Jack stood up and paced back and forth like a coach trying to explain a new play to his team.

"I gathered some of our team together, and we had a sort of summit," Jack said. "We listed everything that we could think of that would lead to creating a 'WOW' customer experience. I mean we listed everything from free ice cream and balloons at the entrance to the store to strolling minstrels. Once we had our list, we crossed off items that were either deemed unnecessary, cost prohibitive, or that we felt we couldn't deliver on 100 percent of the time. Once we eliminated those we had a pretty good list left over. We then worked on how to begin implementing these ideas into our store. We created a timeline knowing we couldn't possibly do everything at once. Our goal was to implement three things at a time. Once we were pretty good at those we added other items from our list. Soon, all the ideas were set in motion.

Jack then crossed the room and stood in front of a

poster on the wall. It was titled "Jack's Place Constitution."

"Because many of our ideas were behavior based, meaning we were asking our associates to speak and act a certain way, we created a constitution to help guide the behavior of our associates," Jack said as John walked over to take a closer look at the constitution.

John went back to his chair and placed his head in his hands amazed and inspired by how much thought was required in putting together a positive customer experience. As he shot up to ask his next question, he realized his world had changed. He was back on the white chaise lounge in the prophet's office.

"That was unexpected!" John blurted out anxiously.

"It was simply time to move on," Stewart replied. "Open your folder to the CEF page. You will see it provides an action plan for you to begin creating your CEF when your previously-scheduled life returns."

"Well, not too soon, I hope," the student replied. "I feel I have so much yet to learn."

"Oh, you do, John. Great marketing involves more pieces that need to be addressed. Do you have any questions on what you need to do to bring your Customer Experience Factor to a new level?"

"I guess I have a lot to figure out," John said with excitement.

"You certainly do. It's a fun process, John, enjoy

Jack's Place Constitution

Be Present; Focus only on the person you're talking to.

When a guest comes within 10 feet, engage them verbally.

Walk guests to the items they ask about.

Own customer complaints from beginning to resolution.

"My pleasure" replaces "You're welcome."

Ask guests if they're finding everything.

Offer pairing options to help the customer make new discoveries.

Execute promotions and displays with excellence.

Treat the customers like guests.

Be nice!

it," Stewart said. "Walk before you run, and do something small each day. Soon you'll be well on your way."

John reviewed the CEF parchment sheet in his folder.

CEF

Delivering a Powerful Customer Experience Factor

Customer Experience Factor - Everyone has a CEF. The word "factor" assumes a number.
The higher the number, the more positive the customer experience.

Deliver on your marketing promise always.

Create a Constitution for your organization establishing "this is how we do it here".

Start with something simple. It doesn't have to be perfect, but it needs to be a living constitution that can evolve over time.

Live it yourself and remind your people every day.

Be relentless with your pursuit of consistency and repetition.

Get your people involved. This is everyone's business, not just yours.

Envision the experience you wish your customer to have. Write it down and allow yourself to be outrageous. Then, start crossing off things you cannot consistently deliver on 100 percent of the time.

Meeting customers' expectations is mandatory. Exceeding expectations pays dividends.

Chapter 7

PROCESS MANAGERS AND PROCESS PARTNERS

The Happy Oyster!

"It's time to move on again, John. Look at the next sheet in your folder and tell me what the label says," Stewart said.

"OK, it says PM/PP," John replied.

"John, out of all the information you have received so far, practicing this will provide the quickest way to improve your life," Stewart said. "The students of mine who have built their empires the quickest are those who embraced the PM/PP."

John was on the edge of his seat. "Lay it on me," he said.

"PM stands for Process Managers and PP stands for Process Partners," Stewart continued. "Process Managers are those people within your organization who are responsible for carrying out your will. It could be as simple as putting a PM in charge of making sure your showroom has a Grand Opening Look Daily or what I call GOLD. Or your PM could be put in charge of something more involved, such as heading the Customer Experience Department. When any task needs to be carried out, you are to assign a PM for that. You may even open it up for people to step forward by asking, 'who will PM that?' The Process Manager must take ownership of that task and either carry it out themselves or empower another to do it. However, if it is not done, the designated PM must take full responsibility for it."

John decided he needed more clarity. "So, it sounds fairly simple. I tell people what to do now. Does simply labeling them a Process Manager make a difference?" he asked.

"When you have a company meeting, do you have circular conversations?" Stewart asked.

"What do you mean?" John replied.

"What I mean is this, John: Do the same topics come up week after week? It could be a dress code issue or a maintenance issue that everyone agrees needs to be fixed in the meeting, but nothing ever gets done," Stewart said.

"Uhm, yeah, that happens to us quite often, and it frustrates me," John admitted.

"Assigning a PM to a task along with a deadline will eliminate your frustration, as long as you hold the PM accountable," Stewart said. "The secret to making this work is appointing the PM in front of their peers. When everyone knows that person is PMing a project, they will respond quicker to the PM's needs. Plus, the appointed PM can't procrastinate. Everyone heard the task and the deadline and can hold that person accountable."

"Process Partners," Stewart went on, "are people outside your organization, independent contractors. You partner with these experts in areas you need to fulfill your vision. For example, you may need signage done for your sales events. Instead of having someone with limited graphic design abilities within your organization dress up the store, partner with an independent graphic artist who handles all signage and direct mail pieces - anything in that area of expertise. They become your Process Partner when it comes to signage. They may work out of their home and produce higher quality, eye-catching point-of-purchase materials than your in-house sales person who happens to know how to do a little graphics work. You should use Process Partners because they are experts at what they do. You pay them only when they're working so you get the best quality while staying within your budget. The key to getting the most out of your Process Partners is to fill them in on your vision. Share with them your system and hold them to it. They'll appreciate that, because other companies they work with never take the time to share their vision."

John wasn't comprehending the significance of the PM and the PP. *There must be more to this,* he thought.

"Forgive me, Stewart. This all makes sense, but it seems almost too simple. That's what's confusing me. I understand having managers in charge of an area of the store, and I already use outside vendors. What am I missing?"

"Everything," the teacher said calmly. "Come, follow me."

"Where are we going this time?" asked John.

"To paradise, my protégé, to paradise," Stewart said.

The Prophet led John to the bookcase. He reached out and grabbed a book titled *Oysters Can Make You Smile.* The Prophet motioned to John to turn around and then pointed to the opposite side of the circular room. There was a door inscribed with a golden, etched sign that read "The Happy Oyster."

"After you," Stewart insisted.

John opened the door. The atmosphere changed the second they crossed the threshold, as they had stepped into a Caribbean-themed restaurant. The sound of reggae, with its distinct steel drums, filled the air. The place was comfortably crowded. The wait staff was dressed in colorful Caribbean attire. A friendly waitress approached holding a tray with hollowed-out coconuts. A small placard on the tray read "Rum Swizzle Punch."

"Welcome to The Happy Oyster—enjoy a rum swizzle!" the waitress kindly insisted. "Oh, hello Stewart!"

"Hi Tracy! And yes, two rum swizzles would be great," Stewart said.

"Who's your cute friend?" Tracy asked with a wink.

"This is John, John Kasten," Stewart replied.

"Hello," said John, blushing like an eighth grader.

"Hi, sweetheart. Would the two of you prefer to sit inside or outside on the Fun Deck?" Tracy asked.

"Why, the Fun Deck, of course. Is there any room?" Stewart asked.

"You know I'll always make room for you, Stewart. I wouldn't be making the tips I'm making if it weren't for you," she said appreciatively.

"You're too kind. You work hard and deserve every cent," he replied.

Tracy led them through the restaurant. The Happy Oyster was decked out in authentic-looking artifacts from the Caribbean's heyday. Pirate treasure chests, tie-dye shirts signed by patrons of the past, nautical decorations and bright colored mosaics were all skillfully placed to create a happy atmosphere. It felt as if you actually were in the Caribbean. Near the inside bar was a massive tank of raw oysters on ice. A large, colorful door had a decorated piece of driftwood above it that read "To the Fun Deck," and in parentheses in small letters, "(No worries, Mon)."

They stepped through the door onto the Fun Deck. People were everywhere taking in the sun. The Fun Deck was situated along a river. About 50 feet from the deck was a large dock with numerous slips for boats. John saw a cement mill across the river and as he looked around he realized that this was a very industrialized area.

They were definitely not south of the border. This could be any Midwestern town. The deck itself had many large exotic looking plants and funky sculptures that enhanced the Caribbean theme. A live reggae band was playing. In a nook was a table for four.

"Here you go," Tracy said as she sat down with them. "Will you be having anything to eat?"

"This is perfect, Tracy. How about an oyster menu? I need to get John introduced to the many ways to eat raw oysters," Stewart replied.

"You got it," Tracy said as she pulled out two small menus. "I suggest the Mango Sliders… they go down quick and leave a sweet satisfying flavor. I'll be right back, sugar."

"So, how do you feel right now, John?" Stewart asked.

"This is exactly what I needed," John said smiling, "This is great!"

"Look around," Stewart said. "This place was a typical bar on the water just eight months ago. It was nice, but it wasn't this fun, vibrant experience. Tony, the owner, fell off his proverbial horse like you did. He, too, was looking to crank up his business. We studied his Market Viability. There were no other Caribbean-themed restaurants in the area. His location along the river made it a natural theme. Sure, he had a good crowd in the summer, but he wanted to be *the* location that offered customers a place where they could feel as if they were on vacation throughout the year."

"He laid out his Customer Experience Factor," Stewart said. "Everything that happened to us the moment we entered the Happy Oyster was choreographed. The wait staff is trained to flatter and engage everyone who steps through the door."

"It seemed so natural and unrehearsed," John said.

"Exactly," Stewart said. "First it may have felt awkward for the staff to meet and greet, but eventually it became natural. Tony fired half his staff during the changeover because they simply couldn't deliver his vision, but what he did in completing his transformation was use a multitude of Process Partners and Process Managers to accelerate the change."

The oysters arrived, delivered by a smiling young man. "Hello, Stewart. Hello, John. I'm Tony. I hear you ordered the Sliding Mango."

"We did, thank you," Stewart responded.

"Nice to meet you. What a great place you have—

congratulations!" John added.

"Thank you," Tony said. "I understand you will be our guests at the DTP meeting?"

"DTP? What does that stand for?" John asked in curiosity.

"That stands for Delivering The Promise," Stewart chimed in. "Yes, Tony, I believe it begins in 45 minutes?"

"That's right. Don't be late or you pay a dollar!" Tony said. "We'll see you boys later."

John and Stewart spent their time enjoying the oysters and the rum swizzle. Since this crazy journey began, John felt as if he had no time to let his mind rest. Now was that time.

The student and teacher enjoyed a few more moments idly bantering back and forth enjoying the day. Then, after awhile, Stewart alerted John that they needed to move on. "It's time to learn more about the fourth phase of using Process Managers and Process Partners," he said. "Let's go meet up with Tony and his team. Follow me."

The teacher led the way across the deck, behind the bar and through a door to a staircase. The staircase led to a conference room that housed a large table and gas fire place. Connected to the room was an outside balcony overlooking the Fun Deck. Above the door leading to the balcony hung a sign that read "Inspect what you Expect." The space was decorated in a nautical motif with a large captain's wheel on the wall complete with an antique compass, anchor and fishing net on the ceiling. The conference table had seven people assembled for the meeting.

"I want to thank everyone for being on time and ready to contribute," Tony said in beginning the meeting. "We have two very special individuals with us today: Stewart our mentor and friend, and his guest, John Kasten."

Everyone said hello and greeted the guests with handshakes and head nods.

"Stewart wanted John to sit in on our meeting to observe how we do things," Tony announced. "Let's begin by introducing our leadership team. Starting to my immediate left is Sharon, our Director of Experience. Sharon Process Manages everything related to sustaining and improving the customer experience. This includes atmosphere, bartenders, chefs, waitstaff and greeters. Next to Sharon is Emily. Emily is an interior designer and an outside vendor. She is a Process Partner who works closely with Sharon overlooking everything to do with the customer experience, including what our team members wear to what containers our drinks are served in. Her most obvious contribution was working to turn this joint into a place right out of a Caribbean resort magazine. Emily understands our vision and works hard to contribute her expertise when we need her."

Emily and Sharon exchanged pleasantries with the new guests. "Next is Justin, our PM for the bartenders. Justin has created a system of entertaining customers. His staff, known as the Crazy Oysters, put on quite the juggling and balancing show behind the bar. Next to Justin is Jackie, our financial genius who is a Process Partner from Gilby and Smith Accounting. She'll be giving a financial report for the last quarter. Next, we have our head chef, Stephen. He process manages the kitchen and makes sure the communication between waitstaff and the cooks are copacetic. Finally, another member on our team is Wally, who is our Process Partner in charge of Internet Relations. He sends out *Sliders*, our weekly e-newsletter that informs clientele of events and bands that will be playing. Plus, he puts together trivia and other interactive fun elements that allow guests to win drink and food coupons."

After the introductions, the meeting continued on a normal path. Jackie started with financials showing the business up 20 percent over the same period last year. Sharon spoke next, reading several e-mails from customers giving kudos to the staff for a great time and how they went over and above their expectations. Wally spoke of how the online newsletter was experiencing an 18 percent increase in unique visitors every month over the previous month. The team discussed new specials and events so Wally could update the information on the Web site.

Every now and then, when an action plan had to be formed, Tony would stop everything and say, "OK, who is going to PM that?" Meaning who was going to step up and take ownership of the initiative at hand. Invariably someone spoke up and said they'd do it. Tony would then say, "When do you think you can get it done?" A defined timeline was set and the conversation moved on. It was amazing to John how fast and efficient the meeting process went. He realized that, except for the 10 minutes that Jackie the accountant talked about financials, the conversation was all about 'how do we make the customer experience better?' It was about leading people and holding each other accountable. The financials, though important, were almost an afterthought.

Tony then looked over at Sharon. "Sharon, what is our Seat and Greet percentage?" he said. "Seat and Greet" referred to the system of having the waitstaff sit down at the table to take orders instead of standing over customers. It was a choreographed ingredient of their system that contributed to the Customer Experience Factor and had been proven to raise check totals.

Sharon gave her report. "My last count was 80 percent Seat and Greet compliant. We are up 10 percent from last month. The newbies are starting to warm up to it. They know that if they don't Seat and Greet, they won't be able to continue to work here. I'm coaching every day."

"Excellent work, Sharon," replied Tony. He then started to remind his team of the dream. "I appreciate everyone raising their game to create the best little Caribbean experience. Remember, if our guests don't feel like they're being treated like they're on vacation, we've failed. It's how we do it here now. With Stewart's help, we've been able to turn an average restaurant into a cash cow. In addition to seeing big increases every month, we're enjoying our jobs more and having fun together. Thanks for Delivering the Promise to our guests and exceeding my expectation for all of you."

John couldn't believe how efficiently the meeting ran and how good everyone was feeling after Tony's praise. His own meetings at work were unorganized, inefficient and boring. Tony's meeting lasted all of 40 minutes. Everyone contributed and left energized. John began to understand the power of the Process Partner and Process Managers. They all felt a part of the company because they understood what their role was, and they felt their contributions were appreciated.

Lost in his thoughts, John suddenly realized he was alone again with Stewart in the white circular office. This time, though, he wasn't taken aback at all from his sudden return to Stewart's office. *"Who cares, the information was great!"* he thought.

"So, the Process Partners are vendors who are treated like they are a part of the organization!" John blurted enthusiastically, as if some ancient secret had been revealed.

"You see, John, everyone has a need to belong," Stewart said. "Treat vendors as an integral part of your company. Extend appreciation and praise when they succeed, and you've gained a valuable and affordable ally. You'll find that they become extremely efficient in advising you because you've let them in, and they know so much about you. They can accomplish their work for you in a fraction of the time. You only pay for what you use. There are no benefits or employment tax for you to pay. Process Partners allow you to work ON your business instead of IN your business. Entrepreneurs need to work ON their vision by sharing and teaching their vision to others."

"And Process Managers are the employees on the inside that get it done!" John declared like a proud student winning a spelling bee.

"They, along with the Process Partners, fulfill your will. They do it because the leader appreciates and respects them. As Brander-In-Chief, your will becomes their will," Stewart said.

"*This is deep and powerful stuff,*" John thought to himself. It was starting to finally sink in.

"If I'm going to lead, I've got to read," John said, recapping what he had so far learned. "I need to become the Brander-In-Chief of my organization. First, I have to determine my Market Viability, which is my position within the market in relation to my competition. Then, I gather my people and develop a constitution of 'this is how we do it here,' defining the Customer Experience Factor. Once the system is defined, I assign Process Managers and Process Partners to fill the needed roles. As Brander-In-Chief, I teach the system and remind everyone of the rules often."

It was really sinking in. The student was maturing in his marketing journey because the first step was understanding the process. The Brander Technician inside of him was slowly changing. He felt it. He was slowly feeling the transformation of reaching his ultimate goal, becoming a Brander-In-Chief.

The Prophet looked on proudly. "You're feeling it, aren't you, John?"

"Yeah!" John replied enthusiastically.

Stewart pressed on. "Tell me, if you could express the feeling you have right now, in a word, what would it be?"

John looked directly into his teacher's eyes. "Confidence. I can finally make confident decisions regarding the direction of my company," he said.

"This is good!" Stewart said encouragingly. "You've learned the hardest part. Now comes the element for long-term success. Getting into the hearts of your customer… developing your MANTRA!"

PM / PP

Process Managers and Process Partners

1. Process Managers are people you employ who take ownership of a task or department.

2. Process Partners are vendors outside the organization who you deem as critical to your success.

3. Appreciate your PM's and PP's. Share your vision with them.

4. Process Partners allow you to work ON your business instead of IN your business.

5. Process Partners can accomplish what you need in a fraction of the time and at a reasonable price. (Especially when treated like a part of the organization.)

6. When partnership is understood, PP's are the accelerators of business.

Chapter 8
MANTRA CONCEPT

Mel's Dinner Theater

"The Mantra Concept is the *feeling* your brand portrays," Stewart said. "It's often first discovered when a person uses the word *'like'* to describe working with you. For example, the first time a customer used a *'like'* phrase with me it came out like this:

"Ya know Stewart, working with you is like being with a good father. Sometimes you challenge me to the point where I just want to give up, but you hold my hand through the process and everything turns out fantastic."

"I then thought about that statement and interpreted it as a feeling of confidence," Stewart said. "After all, isn't *confidence* the core gift that a good father gives a child? If a person doesn't believe they have more confidence in running their business and bettering their life after implementing my marketing system, then I have failed. The desire to give a businessperson confidence with marketing decisions is what drives me every day. Great companies give more to their customers than a product or service. They give them an experience that produces a feeling that often can only be expressed in a *'like'* statement," Stewart explained.

Stewart stood up, walked over to the bookcase and motioned for John to follow him.

"Tell me what you see on the Mantra shelf," Stewart said.

"Well, let's see, books titled with famous people and products," John said.

The books were oddly titled in that some were people and some were products and some were simply emotions: *Walt Disney, Norman Rockwell, Corona Beer, NIKE, Bold, Daring and Rich* were just a few that John spotted on the shelf.

"You need to understand one thing about Mantras," Stewart continued. "They're not slogans. They're how the brand makes a person feel. Go ahead and pick out a book."

John grabbed the book titled *Walt Disney*. He opened the book and found something he wasn't expecting. A childish giggle overcame him. He felt life was perfect and his heart was filled with joy and adventurous curiosity. He then closed the book.

"Whoa, I just felt like a kid again!" John said.

"Ah, hah," laughed Stewart, "Yes, I remember, too. Disney is a brand of youth and adventure with the likes of

Tom Sawyer and Huckleberry Finn. Disney was able to create a world that helped adults be kids again and escape from the serious, chaotic adult-driven world, if only for a moment or a weekend. Go ahead, pick another."

John was really enjoying this lesson. He next grabbed *Corona Beer*. He opened it and immediately felt relaxed, as if he was on a tropical vacation. He closed his eyes and took a deep breath. He could swear he smelled the tropical vegetation of a Mexican getaway, a feeling of relaxation. He didn't want to leave it. Stewart, sensing his reluctance, shut the book for him.

"Man! This is awesome. If I had books like these at home, I wouldn't go anywhere!" John exclaimed.

"Don't you see?" said Stewart calmly. "You surround yourself with these products all the time. Some, several times a month, and others, once every several years. We rely on the brands we trust to make us feel a certain way. We purchase things based on how we believe they'll make us feel, and then, we justify them through logic. In other words, we lead with our heart and follow up with the brain in the form of 'logical' justification. Even a small business can develop its own Mantra. The good ones are already doing it."

"It makes sense," replied John, "but to have someone 'feel' a certain way when they shop my clothing store, I don't know. How do I create a Mantra?"

"A Mantra can show its face in three different ways," Stewart said. "It's either created methodically, it just happens or it is searched for within the organization. It's usually sleeping and needs to be woken up."

"OK…," said John, thoroughly confused.

"The mantra is the most difficult thing for the small business owner to understand," Stewart explained, "but the good news is you may not need to create one because it may already exist within your four walls. Passion is the biggest driver of an already existing Mantra. Brander-In-Chiefs who have a clear vision of the future and clearly portray the values of their company create the Mantra by sheer communication of their vision, and associates buy into it. Grab the money staff, John, we're going for another ride!"

John, excited for the next adventure, placed the book back on the shelf, took hold of the walking staff and closed his eyes.

He opened his eyes moments later to the chatter of people dining. Stewart and John found themselves seated at a banquet table with four other strangers who were busy in conversation. The room was tiered and split into three sections. To his right was a fairly large stage with a red velvet curtain drawn across. This was definitely a theater of some sort. A waitress placed an ice-cold bucket of assorted beverages on their table.

"Thank you, Jessica," Stewart said.

"It's always a pleasure seeing you, Stewart. And you must be John," she said handing him a menu.

"Yes, I am, thanks," John said

"Enjoy the show!" she said.

"Show?" John looked at Stewart.

"Welcome to Mel's Dinner Theater," Stewart said.

"Mel's Dinner Theater? It sounds like a used car lot name, ya know Mel's Used Cars and Tires," John replied jokingly.

"Why, thank you, John, I named it myself," said Stewart like a proud papa. "This is the perfect example of how a Mantra Concept is created through pure passion. Mel and I started this theater together a number of years ago. I left to coach business owners. It's funny because the business world isn't much different than the theater. The product is the show and the representatives are the actors. Mel's is a thriving, profitable dinner theater, which is unheard of in today's theater climate. Some of the hardest businesses to get started in America are restaurants and live theaters. Mel found success doing both through a burning passion to succeed. And he's winning."

One of the ladies extended her hand to Stewart. "Hi, I'm Carol and this is my husband Tom. Our guests are Mary and Sam. Stewart, it's a real honor to have you sit at our table. We've been season ticket holders since back when you were in shows here," she said.

Stewart, in shows? John thought to himself. *What else does this guy do?*

"It's more of an honor for me to sit with you," Stewart exclaimed. "Without your support there wouldn't be a theater."

"Listen," Sam chimed in. "I've seen comedy shows in Vegas and off Broadway. Nothing compares to this. Great harmonies, hilarious story lines and an incredible cast. We never miss a show!"

Tom looked at Stewart, clearly intrigued. "I would love to hear the story of how you and Mel decided to open a dinner theater," he said.

Stewart chuckled to himself and began the story. "Mel and I met doing Community Theater together and instantly became friends," he explained.

John noticed how enraptured the four others were in the story.

Stewart continued, "He called me one day and said, 'Stewart, we're starting a dinner theater and you're going to be Executive Director.' You see, Mel was a partner in a bar/restaurant that had two small banquet rooms with quite a bit of character."

"We remember that!" Carol exclaimed.

"He had the space, but we didn't know what show we could do on an eight-foot by sixteen-foot riser stage. So, we decided to write our own show from scratch. Our first show we wrote on five bar napkins during a long brainstorm over dinner. The rest is history."

John piped in then. "I'm just curious. Being new to this theater, why do you think the theater is so successful?"

"I'll answer that," Mary replied quickly. "Our husbands like to go!"

"It's *like* the Saturday Night Live of theater," Sam chortled. "I'll be as excited to see your reaction as I will the show."

Just then, a jovial gentleman appeared between the drawn curtains and walked out to the front of the stage.

"Welcome to Mel's Dinner Theater!" he said.

"What in the 'Mel' is going on?" The whole crowd chanted back.

"Thanks for asking," Mel said chuckling. "We have a great show for you but before we get started I want to introduce you to Stewart, a special friend of mine who is in the audience tonight. Some of you may even remember him from our first three seasons. Stewart and I started this crazy little theater many moons ago. Stewart, will you please stand up?"

Stewart rose, and the audience applauded him. John couldn't believe this guy. *Marketing master and thespian*, he chuckled to himself.

"Stewart, we had some great times, and I appreciate you! Now, before we get started, let's recite the Mel's Dinner Theater motto," Mel said. "The more we laugh the funnier you are!" the audience yelled out.

"That's right!" Mel said. "So, wait staff bring out the Mel special, and we'll see you in a few minutes!"

The wait staff flooded into the theater carrying bowls of punch for each table. A few minutes later the curtain opened.

The show was brilliant with a mix of a light story line with plenty of hilarious moments and fantastic singing. The soloists were incredible and the harmonies pure joy. By the show's end, the audience unanimously agreed it was terrific and showed their appreciation with a standing ovation. John, too, was standing clapping his hands excitedly. His clapping became extremely loud and out of place as he found himself standing in front of Stewart's couch clapping all by himself.

"I hate it when you do that!" John said, standing in Stewart's white office.

"I know," Stewart smiled back. "Any thoughts on what you experienced?"

"The show was fantastic! What was their Mantra?"

"Well, how did it make you feel?" Stewart said.

"I felt that it was OK to be myself. I was able to forget about my stress for a while and just laugh. Like Sam said, it's the Saturday Night Live of theater."

"And when we first heard that *'like'* statement, Mel and I agreed with it," Stewart said. "That statement was the direction for all future decisions. We asked ourselves: 'What do they do on Saturday Night Live that we could incorporate here?' That's when the pre-show talk by Mel started. We felt the chanting of familiar phrases before every show would fit into the brand and it worked. You see, once that *'like'* statement reveals itself, it's easy to make future decisions on enhancing the brand. All you have to do is be true to it."

"The fundamental values of the brand, which we felt were universal among people, is that everyone just wants to be themselves," Stewart said. "The Mel's Dinner Theater brand pokes fun at life and allows the audience to 'get out of me' for awhile and just laugh."

"The Mantra at Mel's wasn't planned," Stewart said. "Mel and I simply wrote musically-themed shows and funny bits that we felt would have people laughing. We didn't see the big picture in the beginning of all the little sayings that people would be chanting back at us. The Mantra evolved over the years through our passion of doing what we loved to do: sing and make people laugh. There are many small businesses that are a lot less exciting than theater that have taken their passion and infused it into ordinary industries. Eventually, their Mantra evolved through their own passion and vision. Like a self-fulfilling prophecy."

John began to sort through what he had learned so far about the Mantra Concept.

"So, the Mantra is the feeling your brand portrays," he said. "With Corona, it was feeling like being on vaca tion—no worries. The Walt Disney brand had me feeling like a little kid. Mel's Dinner Theater was the feeling of safely letting your hair down and just being yourself while being thoroughly entertained. So, Mantras are created through passion and a personal belief system. Sometimes, they just happen, as in the case of Mel's Dinner Theater. They are expressed by a person who experienced the brand and expressed the feeling through a *'like'* statement, and sometimes they are choreographed by the Brander-In-Chief starting with sharing his or her vision with their associates and then constructing a consistent customer experience through systems of '*this is how we do it here*.' "

"Didn't you say that I may have a Mantra Concept in my organization and not know it?" John asked.

"Why yes, it happens all the time," Stewart said. "Especially when a company has been around awhile. You can do a Mantra discovery right within your four walls. We call the hidden Mantra a sleeping giant. You just need to wake it up!"

"Well, how do I do that?" John asked.

"Take a look in your file, John. Look on your sheet labeled MC," Stewart said.

John went to the desk and grabbed his white file folder. He opened the file and pulled out the paper labeled MC.

The words began magically appearing on the page. Along with a list of notes, appeared a second page; a question naire.

"A questionnaire?" thought John. It was simple, consisting of only eight questions. Stewart grabbed the questionnaire and began to explain it.

"This is what is called an Uncovery form. For great marketing to work within your organization you need input from your associates," Stewart said. "You need their buy-in to implement a successful marketing strategy. They're the ones delivering on the marketing promise, so you need to understand what they already deliver on every day. Whether you know it or not, you are instilling a values system and a feeling within your organization. Positive or negative… you're sending a message. This simple questionnaire will let you know what message you're sending."

"The first question will tell you how you're doing as a visionary coach. Do your associates know the goals of the company? Beyond the financials, are they looking at the big picture? Furthermore, do they know where they fit into this vision? Most associates will respond, 'To make more money?' Money isn't a vision; it's an outcome of executing the vision. The goal is for every person in your organization to know the vision and how they contribute to that vision. Do that and the money will follow."

"Questions two and three define your key strength

Mantra Concept Uncovery Questionnaire

1. What is the long-term vision of your company (what does it look like in 10 years)? What is your contribution to this vision?

2. What three things differentiate your business from the competition?

3. If you only could promote one of these differentiating points, which one would you choose?

4. Which of these factors is/are most difficult for your competition to imitate and why?

5. If you owned the company, what would you change or make better?

6. If you were the marketing director, what advertising message would your potential customers need to hear about your company?

7. Experiencing your brand is like...? (What have customers told you?)

8. If your brand were a car, what would it be and why? Magazine? Restaurant?

in the organization and help you uncover the value system. Your associates are asked to pick a specific strength to help isolate the one thing that makes your store better than your competition."

"The fourth question identifies your Market Viability. Do you have a unique position in the marketplace that's difficult for your competition to duplicate? Question number five gets real as to what can be done better. The sixth question simply confirms their answer to the third question."

"Question seven is trying to dig up those *'like'* statements that may reveal a feeling that exists from your customers' point of view. You may uncover similar *'like'* statements, which will point you in the direction of your Mantra. And finally, question eight takes products that most people are passionate about such as cars, magazines and restaurants and will give you an idea of how similarly your associates relate these brands to your brand. If one associate sees your company as a Lexus and another as a Pinto, you have some disconnect happening."

Stewart then handed the form back to John. "The most important ingredient in executing a successful Mantra Concept Uncovery is honesty. Do you believe your associates feel they can be honest? You can have your people hand in a typed response without their name to increase anonymity. In some circumstances, it works best if a third party administers a verbal Uncovery so body language and vocal tone can be evaluated. That's for you to decide. You must understand your weaknesses as well as your strengths so you can deliver on your current marketing promise."

John reflected on the questionnaire and his experience at the Dinner Theater. "I understand the importance of the Mantra to your marketing message," he said. "My question is this: What if after completing the Uncovery questionnaire there really isn't anything that screams Mantra? How do I begin to create one?"

"That's a good question," Stewart replied. "You will have your strengths to work from. For example, your associates may come back and say that 'selection' is an agreed upon strength. What does 'selection' say and how can that be developed into the Mantra? You first must look at your competition to analyze if the idea of 'selection' is strong enough to hang your hat on."

"Ultimately, how you want your customers to feel when they do business with you will help guide you to the Mantra," Stewart said. "Let's say you decide you want that feeling to be *looking good.* Your conscious goal is for every customer to feel good about themselves because of the attention and wardrobe combinations your associates assist them with. You must clearly communicate this to your employees and then sit down and get them involved.

Ask questions: What do we need to do to consistently deliver this Mantra to our customers? What should our constitution state to help guide our behavior in delivering this *feeling good* Mantra? With the Mantra at the center of what we do, how will this affect future decisions? The Mantra is how you want your customer to feel when doing business with you. It helps guide all future decisions when it is taken to heart and absorbed into your organization. This happens through behavior that is expressed in a constitution that is created for your company by your associates."

"OK," John said, in starting to recap by looking at his Mantra notes. "I explain to my people that I want their honest feedback to a questionnaire which will help us develop a core marketing strategy that revolves around our Mantra. The questionnaire should be typed and handed in without putting their name on the form. Once completed, I see what the majority believes to be true. This will help me understand how my associates see the business. I identify the strengths for which there appear to be consensus and develop these ideas into a core value and Mantra statement. I open this discussion up to the associates, and we create our constitution on how we are going to behave to deliver this Mantra message consistently every day. If I don't like how the information comes back, I clarify what our company believes in and we start from scratch. Regardless of how we come up with the Mantra Concept, we discuss how this Mantra will affect all future decisions."

"It all comes down to practice, John," Stewart said with encouragement. "You didn't learn men's clothing and retail by reading a book. You were instructed first and reminded a thousand times by people before you, but it wasn't until you found success through trial and error by actually doing it in the field that you really started developing a passion and a system for it. My entire process of marketing helps you become a Brander-In-Chief, because a great leader involves people by engaging them to deliver a Customer Experience Factor that wows customers. Gather your people, John. Start with the Uncovery and bring them through every step."

- *Market Viability: What's your position against your competition?*

- *Customer Experience Factor: What's your system within your four walls that delivers the same feeling (Mantra) to the customer every visit?*

- *Process Managers and Partners: Who do you need to help deliver your unique Customer Experience system?*

- *Determine your Mantra Concept and discuss how this will impact future decisions.*

"It's when you step back and look at the big picture of great marketing that you realize this isn't rocket science," said Stewart. "As the BIC, you're a coach asking your players on how to win the game. Then, as the coach, you take the information, formulate a game plan and start calling the plays."

"When you put it like that, you're right—it's step by step," John said. "I just need to focus on one thing at a time and be disciplined, then stay the course."

"I promise you, John," Stewart confirmed, "by making small steps every day, the summit will appear. You will be in control of your business and will be much better able to grow and manage your business for future success. Following your system will become habit and everyone in your life will be happier because the system will give you freedom to do more of the things you like to do, such as making it to your kids' special events and spending more time with your wife. You're making the decision to take control by letting go and empowering others to be a part of your success."

"Alright, John, we're getting close to completing our system. You're on a constant journey in becoming a Brander-In-Chief. You've determined your position within your market category that your competition cannot easily duplicate. You have outlined a clear system of how you do things within your four walls creating a constitution to deliver a consistent Customer Experience, and you've learned how to develop a Mantra, making it the focus of your organization. Now, you need to tell people about you. It's time to advertise!"

MC

Mantra Concept

1. What feeling does your brand portray?

2. How do you want your customers to feel when doing business with you?

3. Good or bad, you most likely already have a Mantra Concept.

4. People who express your Mantra Concept use 'like' statements to express it. Doing business with you is like...

5. A Mantra Concept is discovered through a company's values and sustained through systems of "this is how we do it here".

Chapter 9

SHARE OF VOICE

The Magic Bookcase!

"Without a big-picture understanding of how media works, how can you make good decisions?" Stewart asked.

"You must understand how media works so you can feel confident investing in a plan to get the word out." The teacher then walked over by the bookcase and started running his finger along the row of books labeled SOV. "The sixth stage of our system is Share Of Voice."

Stewart was concentrating hard; it appeared he was looking for a specific book.

"Now where is that bugger?" The books were about media categories such as, TV, radio, Internet, Web site, promotions, cable, satellite, billboards, bus boards, and on and on.

"Ah, here we are!" Stewart said. He smiled and grabbed a book titled, *Media Works*. He placed the book on its side so the spine was on the shelf and the pages faced upward and then shoved the book back into the case. "Stand back," he said.

The two stood back and the entire bookcase started to shift. The center started coming toward them and then opened up revealing a chamber. John could see there were flickering lights and a fog coming from the chamber entrance.

"This is my favorite room!" Stewart said excitedly. "Inside you will see every media that is currently in existence today." The massive bookcase became still. The entrance was big enough to drive a truck through.

"Well, what are we waiting for? After you!" Stewart said.

John stepped through the mist threshold into a world like no other. They were standing on a platform that was a viewing post for the media of the world. It was all so surreal. Every form of communicating with customers was present and all were active simultaneously. Radio station call letters were everywhere. Whatever John focused on was what he could hear. It was magical. It was as if he was the only person who heard sounds from whatever media he looked at.

Thousands of images were floating in the air, and it wasn't just your major media. They were all there: billboards, magazines, vehicle graphics, promotional apparel, sporting events, door hangers, Internet ads - you name it and that medium was present.

This is amazing, John thought. Several minutes passed. John was like a kid engrossed in a video game, tuning out anyone or anything that may interrupt.

"John, focus on me now," Stewart said. "John, if you don't focus on me you won't be able to hear me."

Realizing what he was saying, knowing John could only hear what he was focusing on, Stewart grabbed him by the shoulders and turned him so they were facing each other. Although he was successful in turning the body, John's head remained locked on the images. Stewart gently turned John's face toward him. John looked at Stewart now like a kid seeing a 3-D movie for the first time.
"This is AWESOME!" he exclaimed.

"It absolutely is," the teacher confirmed, "but you need to focus on me in order to hear me. Now, the average person is bombarded by more than 4,000 advertising messages a day. Don't ever let that discourage you, because the average person has only a few favorite mediums they use when looking for information and entertainment. That is the only thing you need to remember."

Stewart then motioned to the field of images suspended in time and space. "How many of the thousands of images out there did you listen to?" he asked.

John looked back toward the sea of media. "Well, at first I was taking it all in, so my attention was focusing on many different mediums for short periods of time," he said.

"Kind of like flipping quickly through TV channels?" Stewart prodded.

"Exactly!" John said. "But then I picked out a few that interested me, and I kept shifting my attention to only those media."

"Exactly my point," Stewart said excitedly. "It's the old 80/20 rule. You spend 80 percent of your time on 20 percent of your choices. However, in media it's more of a 90/10. It's time for you to understand the sixth stage of the marketing process: Share of Voice. Share of Voice means that compared to your competition, who is getting the biggest share of a target audiences' attention? The old advertising rule stated that you needed to dominate your competitor in your spending levels to get your share of an audience. The new rule is this: What you spend has little to do with Share of Voice. Instead, it has everything to do with how well you're concentrated in any particular medium and the strength of your marketing message."

"There are only three rules you need to remember when putting together your Share Of Voice strategy," Stewart said. "I've already told you about the first one. Out of all the media out there, the average person spends about 90 percent of their media exposure time on less than 10 percent of their total choices. We'll call that the 90/10 rule.

That's good, because that means you don't need to be everywhere with your Share Of Voice media placement strategy to be successful. Now, let's learn the second and third most important rules that go hand in hand with this first rule."

"John, do you see that sports stadium off to your right?" Stewart said as he pointed to a floating stadium picture in the sea of media.

"There it is! Clustered among those radio station call letters," John called out as if playing a game of I Spy.

"You got it." Stewart said. "Now, I want you to completely focus on it. Allow it to grow bigger and come toward you as you shut out everything else but that stadium image."

"OK, I'll try." John said as he focused with all of his concentration. And sure enough, just as Stewart promised, the image started coming toward him. "It's getting bigger and coming toward me!" John exclaimed.

"Good, John, don't lose sight of it," Stewart said. "Allow it to grow and don't stop concentrating."

The image continued to grow until it was finally upon them. John blinked for just a moment, and suddenly, he realized that he and Stewart were standing on the field of a major sporting complex. The fans were packed in the seats. There must have been close to 100,000 excited sports fans, and John felt a little uncomfortable standing in the middle of the playing field.

"Don't feel alarmed, John, they can't see us,"

Stewart said. "I brought you here to make a point. I'm going to show you two scenarios to illustrate a powerful lesson when it comes to media. How powerful would it be to have the opportunity to spend one minute telling all these people something unique about your store?"

"Are you kidding me?" John said. "It would be awesome. If only 1 percent of this audience shopped my store, that would be 1,000 new customers. Let me at 'em!"

"OK," Stewart said. He then snapped his fingers and John found himself on the stage in some sort of arena. The space was much smaller than the massive 100,000-seat stadium he was standing in just moments before.

"Where are we?" he asked.

"We are in a multi-purpose arena," Stewart said. "Here you will find everything from basketball to rock concerts. There are 10,000 seats in this complex. OK, what is more powerful: to speak one time for one minute to 100,000 people in the stadium OR to speak to the same audience for one minute 10 times in this 10,000 seat arena?

John thought about that: *If I speak 10 times to the same 10,000 people I am still only talking to the same 10,000 prospects. However, if I speak to the 100,000 folks in the stadium even once that's 10 times more people.* "I'll go with the stadium," John said with confidence.

"Then, you are deciding to go for a massive reach over the frequency of talking to the same audience, be it much smaller, 10 separate times. Is that correct?" Stewart asked.

"Yeah, as I said, if only 1 percent of the stadium did business with me, that would be 1,000 new customers as apposed to 1 percent of 10,000 which would be 100 people."

"This is where you are mistaken," Stewart said as he waved his staff. They were now back in his office, John on the couch and Stewart in the chair. Stewart went on as if nothing had happened. "Most business owners would agree with you. They believe that reach beats frequency, but it simply isn't true. Your prospects are busy people. Think about what goes on in our daily lives: children, events to get to, volunteerism, work, deadlines and stress. It is more important to remind someone of something over and over again than to instruct only one time. We learn through repetition and consistency. Therefore, rule No. 2 is: It's better to reach 10 percent of the people many times than 100 percent of the people one time. The third rule is a simplification of the second rule: Frequency beats Reach every time."

John reached for the Share of Voice sheet in his folder, and like the former lessons the rules magically revealed themselves.

"OK, so I have the three rules," John said, "but could you share with me how I use these rules to create a media strategy for my business?"

"Your business is men's clothing. I'd say that's a very specific audience," Stewart said. "Men can be reached through men's magazines, and they typically watch and listen to sports programming. How many media in your market, if we just focused on television, radio and newspaper, do you believe reach your target audience?"

"A lot!" John gasped. "About three dozen cable channels. Every broadcast TV station has programming that reach men. Newspapers certainly reach a percentage of my target, and I would say there are about five radio stations that cater to my target audience."

"You certainly can't afford to be frequent in all these media, can you?" Stewart asked.

"Certainly not!" John said.

"Then, it's best to start with one and saturate that media. For example, own the listeners on one radio station by placing 10 ads a day, three days a week for 52 weeks. This audience is loyal to the station's programming and will hear you sharing your persuasive message over and over again. Your Share of Voice on that station will be outstanding. When your sales begin to grow you can either add another day to that station or look at one TV program. Remember that with TV, people are loyal to programs not stations, so pick a program that your target audience enjoys watching and make sure your commercial is there frequently. The audience that is loyal to the program will see your ad over and over again. It will appear as if you're advertising 'all the time' when in reality you may be only advertising on that program. Frequency is built by focusing your resources on a few media rather then spreading it out across many."

"I think I'm understanding you," John said. "What you're saying, if I'm understanding you right, is that I should be loyal with one or two radio stations by being on them frequently and consistently to build frequency. Then on TV, I would need to be loyal to specific programs that my target audience watches."

"By George, he can be coached," Stewart said. "And to build greater frequency on TV, when starting, pick only programs that air five days a week because the people who are loyal to that program will see you over and over again. They will begin to understand your difference and eventually take action and shop you."

"Then, my Customer Experience Factor will compel them to buy!" John added.

John really was beginning to understand this marketing philosophy. The Prophet's marketing system was being replayed in his brain like a movie on fast forward.

- *FIRST: Become a Brander-In-Chief and take the time to work ON my business and not always IN it. Hold people accountable and create a real vision for the future of my company.*

- *SECOND: Market Viability— Create a defined position in the marketplace within my product category. What am I going to be known for?*

• *THIRD: Make the Customer Experience Factor a priority by creating a system of "This is How we Do it Here" that governs the day-to-day behavior of my associates. Get my people involved—they'll help me do it.*

• *FOURTH: Find the right Process Managers within my company to carry out my will. Also look for Process Partners outside my organization who specialize in the areas I am weak. Embrace these people and make them feel a part of the business and share with them the vision for the company.*

• *FIFTH: Develop our Mantra Concept... the feeling people will have when shopping our store.*

• *SIXTH: Take our message and create a Share Of Voice strategy understanding that Frequency beats Reach every day. Remember that people are only loyal to less than 10 percent of their total media choices, so if I stay consistent and frequent on a particular media, I can build frequency quickly and affordably.*

John, referring back to his opened folder, removed the final page. As with the other pages in his folder, it too had a label on top. This page, however, consisted of only one letter, a large P.

"Stewart, I see that one page remains in this folder.

This big P. What does it stand for?"

"Ahh, yes," Stewart said with a twinkle in his eye. "The very essence of success. This stage represents the fundamental truth that turns paupers into kings and deck hands into captains… PASSION!"

SOV

Share Of Voice

Share of Voice Rules:

1. The 90/10 rule- People have many options for their attention with media. However, they spend 90 percent of their media time on less than 10 percent of the total media choices, and they stick with the same media day after day.

2. It's better to reach 10 percent of the people many times than 100 percent of the people one time.

3. Frequency beats Reach every time.
It's more important for people to be reminded than instructed.

Chapter 10
PASSION

The Brander-in-Chief Club!

A chill overcame John as he reflected on Stewart's words. He looked at the paper in his hand and stared thoughtfully at the letter P. As he studied the page, he noticed the letter was transforming into something, but he could not make out what it was. Slowly, the letter became larger and filled the page, then shrunk down again, twisting and morphing into something. Yes, it was becoming clearer… of course, a key! The letter P turned into some sort of ornate looking key. John looked up at Stewart bewilderedly.

"Well, don't just sit there. Grab the key. We have one more stop," Stewart said, getting up and heading toward a specific section of the white round office wall.

John looked back down on his paper and there was a real key sitting on the page. It was artistically ornate with a lot more substance than the old skeleton keys he remembered as a youth from his grandmother's house. John grabbed the key and placed his folder on the couch. He stood up and followed.

They ended up in another section of the circular room. Until now, there had always been doors that appeared, bookshelves that opened or something else that was spectacular. Now, they were simply standing at a blank white wall.

"Where did I put that?" Stewart mumbled to himself. He was feeling all over his body for something. John watched with intense curiosity.

"Ah, here it is!" Stewart said. The teacher pulled out a black marker. He bent over slightly and drew a small symbol on the white wall.

"There you go," Stewart said, motioning at the tiny artwork.

"There I go… what?" John said confused.

"That's a keyhole, John. Place your key into the keyhole," Stewart said.

Of course it is, John amused himself at the thought. *Why should it surprise me after the wild journey that I've been on?*

"C'mon, C'mon, we have people waiting!" Stewart urged. John did as he was asked, and as the key approached the crude black markings a real keyhole mysteriously appeared. John inserted the key and turned it clockwise.

As he turned the key, a large wooden door appeared in the formerly plain white wall. It was large and had a foreboding look. It was made of solid oak with ornate carvings decorating its surface. John opened the door.

John and Stewart entered a large conference room with a large oval table. Sitting around the table were familiar people. Tony, from the Happy Oyster; crazy Mel from the dinner theater and Jack from Jack's Place grocery store. The three stood up and greeted the entering party.

"Welcome young Brander-In-Chief to the world of working ON your business versus IN your business," Jack said.

John entered the room. It was as if they were in the boardroom of some law firm with rich hardwoods representing success and wealth. On the walls were portraits of great entrepreneurs: Colonel Sanders, Mary Kay, Ray Kroc, Bill Gates, Liz Claiborne, Henry Ford, Andrew Carnegie and others.

Jack motioned for everyone to sit down while he remained standing. "Ya know, there are only two things these entrepreneurs have that most people don't have—courage and the ability to express their vision. There are many great business owners out there who are successful, but have not yet tapped their greatness and true potential because of fear of the unknown. The folks around this table and represented on the wall had the courage to move forward. They provided a clear vision of the big picture.

They kept their people focused on it daily and began doing small things right every day, which eventually developed into their vision being fulfilled, such as the McDonald's franchise or the innovative thinking that created Microsoft. You may think because you own a small men's clothing store you can't become great. Whether you think you can or whether you think you can't… you're right."

"Those of us gathered in this room don't have national companies. Greatness doesn't always correlate with size. Greatness comes in the form of making a profit and creating a cohesive team through coaching others to be their best, all while creating a healthy balance at home. Only a Brander-In-Chief can do this."

"Courage and vision are the backbone of America and the entrepreneurial spirit," Jack continued. "Without it, we become average. You have been given a gift, John. The elements of a great brand lay within the Marketing System that Stewart shared with you. It's now up to you to add courage and vision into the mix and become passionate about creating that unique Customer Experience Factor within your four walls. Preach the system and walk and talk it every day. Turning your strong intentions into action is something we can't give you. Only you can do that. We will, however, give you this." Jack held out a small package for John to accept.

It was a small shiny gold box. He recognized it from Jack's office. He remembered seeing it when Jack opened the safe in his office. At the time, Jack handed him the Happy Meal box and this small gold box remained in the safe. Stewart sat beside his student.

"Go ahead," Stewart said. "Open it." John reached out, picked up the shiny mystery box and opened it. Not knowing what to expect, John removed its simple contents: a golden whistle attached to a lanyard. The rest of the group pulled out their golden whistles and placed them around their necks.

"From this day forward, you are no longer a boss," Jack said, taking the whistle and placing it around John's neck. "You're a coach. And it's your job to take what you have learned and develop a game plan. Once you've developed your 'this is how we do it here' system, your next duty is to act upon it. Hold your people accountable to stick to the game plan. Sure, opportunities will come and your strategy may need to be adjusted, but the fundamental values of your game will not. Coach the system and remind your players often about how, together, you're going to win the game. Wear this golden whistle to remind yourself and your people that you are the coach, and you will be coaching your people every day for one reason… to get results, to win!"

John looked at his whistle with the empowering feeling that he could accomplish anything. He was convinced he must take action on everything he learned. By working ON his business and not IN it, his business would grow, and more importantly, his family would become closer. By working on his business creating a powerful "this is how we do it here" system, he could leave the business knowing everything would remain just how he left it when he returned.

Yes, his business would grow in his absence, he thought. *The System will set me free to dedicate more time to my wife and kids. I'll not only coach my employees,* John thought. *"I'll coach my kids basketball team! Dinner around the table every night promptly at six."* He could see it; he could feel it. While in this visionary state, his physical world was changing. He was feeling dizzy and cold. Voices starting ringing out…

"Dude, you alright? He's over here!" yelled Paul. Frank came running over with his gun. John opened his eyes to find himself lying on his back. The sun had set. It was dusk on this brisk November day. He could see the fort that he fell from above and his gun lying about 10 feet away. He slowly sat up. Frank came up and looked him straight in the eyes with a serious look.

"John, do you know who you are and what day it is?" Frank asked.

"Yeah, I do, Frank. I'm John and today is a new day!" replied John.

Frank was a little confused on the last part but could see that their buddy would be fine.

"Man, you had us worried when you didn't return to camp. It's not like you to miss a meal and a cold beer.

What's this?" Frank asked. A gold whistle hung around John's neck. John was at first stunned to look down and see the whistle, but immediately his face changed to reassurance.

"Oh yeah, I found it in the woods," he said.

"It looks brand new," Frank said bewildered.

"It is new," John smiled. *The student was now the teacher; the player was now the coach,* he realized.

The Ad Prophet's Marketing System

1. Brander-in-Chief – Work ON your Business by sharing your vision with everyone you meet, becoming an ambassador for your business.

2. Market Viability – Create a niche within your product category.

3. Customer Experience Factor – A consistent customer experience created through a "this is how we do it here" system guiding associate behavior.

4. Process Managers / Process Partners – The talented people who complete the tasks necessary for carrying out your vision.

5. Mantra Concept – The feeling people have when doing business with you.

6. Share of Voice – Remember the Share of Voice Rules for maximizing your advertising investment.

7. Passion – Go to work with purpose!

Chapter 11

15 MONTHS LATER...

I'll take a suit to go, please!

The fact was John Kasten did take what he learned to heart. He was now three months away from opening a second location in a community located 30 miles from his current store. Business was booming. It didn't happen overnight, however. Quite honestly, in the beginning some of his associates created a lot of internal stress as they learned the new system. They all didn't buy into this new vision for the company. He had to let a few of them go. On the flip side, his new way of working attracted some of the best talent in the area.

After John's "out of body" experience, he began immediately envisioning what he wanted the customer to experience on the sales floor. He then went to his staff and described his vision for the future. Some pushed away, but the majority found a new excitement in the store. He challenged them to come up with a system of how they would consistently deliver a “gotta talk about it to my friends” customer experience. In about two months, the system was complete. They simply named it the Big Blast!

You see, BIG was an acronym for associate behavior when the customer entered the store:

"B" stood for Be Present. The staff agreed that being present with a guest meant greeting them upon entry with a handshake and a smile.

“I” stands for “In-gage” immediately. Based on the word Engage, every associate is to notice something special about a guest. For example, if they have cute children. Or if they're wearing nice glasses. Or if they have their favorite sports team jacket on. Anything that makes the interaction personal to each individual is fair game.

"G" stood for Gather Information. It's important to identify why the guest stopped in so they can be catered to promptly and accurately.

It was important to find out what the customer was looking for: sport coat, suit, tux rental, casual or formal? The team agreed that if the guest was looking for a suit or sport coat, once the selection has been made a second associate shows them a BLAST. This stands for Belts, Leathers, Accessories, Shirts and Ties. John had this system typed into a constitution that all the associates signed. This agreement was the foundation of his “this is how we do it here” system that produced a consistent and positive customer experience.

His business was rarely slammed, and that’s how he liked it. Steady wins the race and allows for sufficient time with each customer. On average, four customers were being waited on at a time. It was a nice pace, much different from the days of waiting and praying for customers to show up. As he panned the showroom floor he saw at least two associates, sometimes three, assisting guests. *Oh, yeah, that was a new way of looking at customers... they’re guests.*

One day when John was doing his routine floor rounds, an associate approached him and said, “John, there’s a gentleman asking to talk to the Brander-In-Chief.” John thought about the phrasing of the request. *Could it be?* John’s eyes grew wide in excitement.

John was led to a gentleman whose back was to him. He was dressed in a white suit and was looking at accessories with an associate. “May I help you?” John asked. The man did not turn. Instead he reached for a stylish white hat, and while placing it on his head said, “I just wanted to congratulate the man responsible for the best suit-buying shopping experience I’ve ever had.” Then, the man turned around.

“Stewart!” John said in humorous amazement.

"The very one," said the man with a sheepish grin. "You've come a long way, John. When I do my 15-month assessment of students, this is exactly what I hope to find."

"I have so much to share with you!" John said like a child at Christmas. The other associates were intrigued at their mentor's reaction to the man in white.

"Everyone, this is Stewart. He was instrumental to our success," John said. The associates introduced themselves and shook Stewart's hand.

"Stewart, do you have some time for a huddle up?" John said with a fire of delight.

"That's what I'm here for," he said with a nod. John led Stewart to his office. John's office looked like that of a head coach. Behind his desk was a chalkboard with circles and lines illustrating his vision strategy. Each associate had a clipboard hanging along the wall and even a locker for storing personal items. And, of course, around his neck was the golden whistle.

Stewart was pleased at the presentation. "You've really come a long way," he said. "I've had many students, John, but you have taken the idea of being the Brander-In-Chief to the ultimate extreme. I love it!"

John beamed like a proud parent hearing praise about a child. "Stewart, you changed my life!" he said. "I have more time at home. I leave at six o'clock at night and arrive at nine every morning. I work two Saturdays a month but only five hours. I coach my kids sporting events and make every game and every concert. My staff understands the system, and is working hard to live it every day. I'm alive again!"

"Explain how you created your system to me," Stewart said enjoying his friend's enthusiasm. He had seen many students take the system and build empires. He had also seen some who returned to their unproductive ways. He was pleased that John took his training from intentions to actions. John stood up and went to the chalkboard and wiped it clean. He then began explaining how he carried out the marketing system Stewart taught him.

"I put myself in my customer's shoes, trying to understand what they really want," John began as he paced back and forth like a player addressing his coach, "I interviewed my staff one-on-one. Through open dialogue, we settled on the fact that the thing all guys really want when it comes to clothing is to pay a fair price and leave with the confidence that they look good."

"The first thing I did was replace salaries with commissions for the sales associates." John said while drawing out circles and X's to illustrate his system. "Then we worked hard at creating a consistent Customer Experience Factor. We call it the BIG BLAST."

"When guests leave the dressing room, they are led to a display table where two associates can assist them," John said. "This system works because I have built a transparent organization built on trust and honesty. Our associates rotate between foundation (suits and sport coats) and accessories selling."

Stewart sat back in his chair and smiled. The customer experience John described to him was exactly what Stewart experienced in the 35 minutes shopping his store.

"You truly have grasped the concept of systems, John," Stewart proudly said to his good student. "Now, tell me, did you sign up some Process Partners?"

John nodded quickly, "Oh, yes! The people I rely upon behind the scenes were amazed when I first shared with them my long-range goals. I continually remind them how instrumental they are to our success. I continue to share with them my expectations. I am saving a ton of money partnering with these outside experts. They consistently over deliver what I'm paying for!"

Stewart nodded in agreement. "That's because you brought them into your world and told them that they matter to you. Did you know that Mother Theresa was quoted as saying: *'People crave appreciation more than food?'* She would know. It's true, and you're giving it to them. I'm extremely proud and excited for you. If every business owner did what you're doing the national statistic for failed enterprises would plummet. Plus, they would have happier and more productive lives. Unfortunately, there will always be Brander Paranoids out there. They'll continue to not trust and demean others in order to raise themselves up. It's sad but true. The great news is we have more Brander Technicians and Brander Phobics who need to learn how to lead their organizations to greatness and who are in great positions to become successful Brander-In-Chiefs."

"How did you discover your Mantra Concept? How clearly have you defined it?" Stewart asked prodding John.

"My first objective was to create a system that would deliver a positive Customer Experience Factor." John said. "When we really started humming, I would hear things from our guests. Whenever I heard a *'like'* statement, my ears would perk up. I then asked my staff to report all *'like'* statements to me as soon as they heard them. We heard statements such as: *You're like a real guys hang out, I know I'm going to look good so I don't need to bring along my wife.* OR *It feels like I'm working with a personal trainer for suits.* Statements such as these are what helped us form our Mantra Concept: "Permanent Attention".

"The day we quit being permanently fixed on each and every guest's needs when they walk into our store is the day our competition takes money out of our register," John said. His passion was evident during his well thought out explanation of his "this is how we do it here" plan of action.

"Permanent Attention, I like that and agree with it after my first experience in your store. I was completely attended too and was fully engaged by your staff. They truly cared about what I was looking for," Stewart remarked.

"Tell me, John, about your advertising. How did you set up your Share Of Voice strategy?" Stewart asked.

"Our advertising is working like a charm. One of the Process Partners I pursued was a marketing firm. I interviewed many and chose the one whose values closely aligned with mine. They're my caddy, and I am very much involved because I 'swing the club' on final decisions. It's my job to say 'yes and no' and to provide feedback. It's great. Before this firm, I relied on the media representatives for help and they were great. I picked one station that catered mostly to men and put my entire budget there. People started to notice my consistency and slowly came in to explore the store. We converted them into raving fans, one customer at a time. It worked!"

Stewart was amazed at how well his student listened and implemented. "It's one thing to be instructed, but it's quite another to take action. You did it and you're doing it, John!" Stewart said.

John began thinking of his friends: Frank and Paul. Their businesses have extreme ups and downs. Complete inconsistency. Feeling fortunate with his newfound freedom, John looked at Stewart and asked,

"Stewart, any chance you could coach my buddies to learn this powerful system of yours? I know they could use your help." John asked.

Stewart stood up and placed his hat upon his head. "John, when the student is ready, the teacher will arrive. You're a Prophet now. First, you were the student, and now, you're the teacher. The player is now the coach. You've been given a gift. Share it with others."

Stewart reached inside his coat and pulled out what appeared to be a miniature staff. He tapped it twice, and it instantly expanded into its original full length. "My work here is done," Stewart said with a twinkle in his eye.

"So, when will I see you again?" John asked, smiling.

"Why, when I need a new suit, naturally!" Stewart replied. And with that he placed both his hands on the staff and disappeared.

On the chair where the Ad Prophet had just sat appeared a small red piece of silk ribbon. John recognized it as being nearly identical to the piece he had found within the Happy Meal box in Jack's office. He reached in his top desk drawer to find that original piece which read, "The System Is the Solution." He gently picked up this second piece and sure enough, there was writing on it as well:

15 Months Later...

Afterword:

When I really think about it, the inspiration to write this book started when I was coming off of five years in media sales and was one year into my new advertising agency. I realized that I didn't truly understand marketing. I knew, however, what it wasn't. It wasn't just commercials on TV and radio. It wasn't having a jingle. It wasn't just a good creative message.

I made it my crusade to understand what solid organizations that I felt delivered an amazing customer experience understood. I also attended multiple seminars led by various marketing gurus to uncover the key elements to great marketing. I discovered that all the businesses I studied that did marketing well had seven distinct ingredients that were alive in the organization. I put these seven ingredients into a system called the PROPHIT Marketing System and tested it over a two-year period with various clients. Sure enough, the clients who took my system to heart saw sales increase and profits rise. Prophit Marketing combines the words "prophet" and "profit," which is based on the idea that one must be a prophet to make a profit. My journey has been one like a Prophet in that first I was the student then the teacher.